SARDIS:
TWENTY-SEVEN YEARS
OF DISCOVERY

PAPERS PRESENTED AT A SYMPOSIUM SPONSORED BY **THE ARCHAEOLOGICAL INSTITUTE OF AMERICA**, CHICAGO SOCIETY, AND **THE ORIENTAL INSTITUTE OF THE UNIVERSITY OF CHICAGO**; HELD AT THE ORIENTAL INSTITUTE

MARCH 21, 1987

EDITED

BY

ELEANOR GURALNICK

CHICAGO 1987

ISBN: O-9609042-1-2

Library of Congress Card Number: 87-070637

TABLE OF CONTENTS

The photographs, maps and drawings that are reproduced in this publication were provided by the Harvard-Cornell Sardis Expedition also known as the Archaeological Exploration of Sardis, the Oriental Institute Museum of the University of Chicago, and the respective authors. It is to be understood that in providing these illustrations both institutional representatives and authors have exercised their personal responsibility in providing the Editor with all necessary permissions to publish these photographs, maps, and drawings and proper attributions to identify their sources.

GUSTAVUS F. SWIFT, JR.

This volume of papers on ancient Sardis is dedicated to the memory of Gustavus F. Swift, Jr.

Swift was a leader in the Chicago Society of the Archaeological Institute of America for some twenty-nine years, and was serving as Treasurer of the national AIA at the time of his death in 1976. He initiated many innovations at the Oriental Institute after his appointment as its first full-time Curator. Here it is appropriate to record briefly his involvement with the archaeological exploration of Sardis.

Gustavus F. Swift, Jr. served as senior American archaeologist and administrator for the Archaeological Exploration of Sardis from 1960 until his death in 1976. He was an honorary research fellow for Sardis at Harvard University.

Swift spent eight summers in the field, and among his many discoveries was the Lydian marketplace that existed during the reigns of Kings Gyges and Croesus. The finds of the House of Bronzes (HOB) or the market area were of great importance to both the economic and cultural history of the period. He presented a paper on the market area at the Tenth International Congress of Classical Archaeology in Izmir; he published preliminary reports of the work annually in the years 1961–1967 and in 1969 and 1971; and Professor Andrew Ramage is currently working on a manuscript examining Swift's finds as well as those involving the marketplace made since.

The deep sounding tests Swift made while in the field established the stratification and dated Sardis back as far as the mid-second millennium B.C. Prior to these soundings Sardis was thought to be occupied only as early as the Iron Age.

FOREWORD

The "Twenty-five Years of Discovery at Sardis" exhibition at the Oriental Institute Museum of the University of Chicago consists mainly of photographs, drawings, watercolors, and text panels, documenting the field excavations and discoveries at this important site in southwestern Turkey. The exhibition was created by the Harvard-Cornell Sardis Expedition with the support of the National Endowment for the Humanities. It will be seen in 13 museums across the United States.

Sardis, which first attained prominence as the capital of the Lydian Kingdom in the seventh century, B.C., was the western terminus of the Persian Royal Road from Susa described by Herodotus. It remained one of the great cities of Asia Minor until the late Byzantine period. Discoveries at Sardis include extensive gold refineries (Croesus was the last of the Lydian kings) and the immense Roman gymnasium complex, one hall of which was given over to the Jewish community in late Roman times and converted into an enormous synagogue over 200 feet long.

The importance of the discoveries at Sardis and the presence of the exhibition together inspired the decision to present the symposium, Sardis: Twenty-seven Years of Discovery, and the publication of its scholarly papers. Conceived as a cooperative effort, the symposium brought the Oriental Institute and the Archaeological Institute of America together to provide a public forum for the outstanding scholars who gathered together in Chicago to share their knowledge.

ACKNOWLEDGEMENTS

The symposium on Sardis was made possible by grants from the Symposium Committee of the Archaeological Institute of America, the Turkish Consulate General in Chicago, the Illinois Humanities Council, and the National Endowment for the Humanities, with additional funding from the Illinois General Assembly, The Harvard-Cornell Sardis Expedition, the Oriental Institute of the University of Chicago, and Mrs. Gustavus F. Swift, Jr. Publication of the symposium papers was supported by the Archaeological Institute of America and its Chicago Society, the Turkish Consulate General in Chicago, the Sardis Expedition Fund at Cornell University and, and several Archaeological Institute of America members including Robert D. Biggs, Elizabeth Gebhard, Albert Haas, and Alex Tulsky. Many individuals made significant contributions to the success of the symposium. Gretel Braidwood, in her capacity as Membership Secretary for the Oriental Institute, contributed to the planning and organization of the event. She coordinated a myriad of activities on behalf of the museum staff in cooperation with the cosponsoring Chicago Society and personally dealt with an unending series of essential details. Joan Barghusen coordinated support activities contributed by museum volunteers. These and many other support services generously contributed by members of the Oriental Institute are appreciated. Above all, I wish to thank Dr. Janet H. Johnson, Director of the Oriental Institute, for her strong and continuous support for the jointly-sponsored symposium, thus assuring its ultimate success. [The officers of the Chicago Society gave generously of their time and talent, likewise contributing to the success of the occasion.) My thanks go in particular to Robert Biggs, Peter Kosiba, and Boris Spiroff. Two members of the Sardis Expedition made notable contributions to the publication. Jane Scott provided nearly all of the illustrations appearing in this book from the Sardis Achive. Nancy H. Ramage provided original drawings for the cover design. John Larson, archivist of the Oriental Institute Museum, granted permission for its silver stater of Croesus to enhance the title page. Very special thanks are due to Roberta Gutman, whose outstanding editorial skills added to the clarity and readability of the papers and to David Baird for preparing the final camera-ready copy. Last, but not least, special thanks go to the speakers and authors, for it is the participants, above all, who made the symposium and this publication possible.

Eleanor Guralnick
Symposium Project Director
The Chicago Society

NOTES ABOUT THE AUTHORS

DAVID GORDON MITTEN, Ph.D.

James Loeb Professor of Classical Art and Archaeology, Departments of Classics and Fine Arts, Harvard University, Cambridge, Massachusetts. A participant in the Archaeological Exploration of Sardis since 1959, his involvement has been in many capacities. He was Assistant to the Directors, 1963; Assistant Field Director, 1964–69; and has served as Associate Director since 1976. His publications on Sardis include contributions to many preliminary excavation reports, several reports on the prehistoric finds from the region near the Gygean Lake with Güldem Yügrüm, and portions of the prehistoric section of the forthcoming report, *Pottery, Prehistoric to Turkish*. His other publications include the *Catalogue of Classical Bronzes*, Museum of Art, Rhode Island School of Design, Providence (1975). With S. F. Doeringer, he edited and contributed to *Master Bronzes from the Classical World* (1967) and *Art and Technology: A Symposium on Classical Bronzes* (1971).

ANDREW RAMAGE, Ph.D.

Professor, Department of the History of Art and Archaeology, Cornell University, Ithaca, New York. He is currently Associate Field Director of the Harvard-Cornell Sardis Expedition and Editor, with Jane Scott, of the Sardis publications. He has been continuously associated with the Sardis Expedition since 1965, and has been in the field for all but two seasons since. Starting as an excavator, he has progressed through a series of responsibilities to his present ones involving both research and supervision. Lydian Sardis is his main professional interest. His book, *Lydian Houses and Architectural Terracottas* (1978) is in print and two others are forthcoming, *House of Bronzes: Lydian Trench* on the Early Iron Age and Prehistoric explorations and the final excavation report, *Pactolus North*, which includes the report on the Lydian gold refining installations.

MACHTELD J. MELLINK, Ph.D.

Professor, Department of Classical and Near Eastern Archaeology, Bryn Mawr College, Bryn Mawr, Pennsylvania, and past president of the Archaeological Institute of America. She has been dedicated to the archaeological exploration of Anatolia since 1947 when she joined the expedition investigating Tarsus.

Four years later, in 1950, she joined the group exploring at Gordion. Since 1963 she has directed the excavations at Emalı. For more than thirty years she has annually compiled "Archaeology in Asia Minor" for the *American Journal of Archaeology*. This is a detailed summary of ongoing investigations and discoveries for all periods from the prehistoric through the Byzantine. Her many publications on Anatolian topics include, *Hittite Cemetery at Gordion* (1956), *Frühestufen der Kunst* with J. Philip (1974), and four forthcoming volumes, *Prehistoric Excavations at Emalı*, *Painted Tomb Chambers at Emalı*, *The Smaller City Mound at Gordion*, and *Wall Paintings from Gordion*. Also, she edited the published papers of a symposium held at Bryn Mawr as *Troy and the Trojan War* (1986).

NANCY H. RAMAGE, Ph.D.

Associate Professor and Chairman, Department of Art History, Ithaca College, Ithaca, New York. Having joined the Sardis Expedition in 1964 as a draftswoman, her interests in the arts at Sardis led to coauthorship with G. M. A. Hanfmann of *Sculpture from Sardis* (1978). The forthcoming publication, *Mainland Greek Pottery from Sardis*, will include her chapter, "Attic Pottery," reflecting her more recent contributions to the understanding of the site. Currently she is preparing yet another manuscript on an area known as Pactolus Cliff, which was excavated early in the Sardis-Cornell explorations. During twenty-three years of association with the Sardis Expedition, she has also published a number of articles on sculpture and pottery excavated at Sardis as well as on other topics.

JANE C. WALDBAUM, Ph.D.

Professor and Chairman, Department of Art History, University of Wisconsin, Milwaukee. Since 1968 she has worked with the Sardis Expedition in a series of capacities from excavator to Editor and Research Fellow. She is the author of *From Bronze to Iron* (1978) on the transition from the Bronze Age to the Iron Age in the Eastern Mediterranean, *Metalwork from Sardis: The Finds from 1958-1974* (1983), *A Survey of Sardis and the Major Monuments Outside the City Walls* (1975) with G. M. A. Hanfmann, and of a number of papers on a variety of topics relating to Sardis.

FIKRET K. YEGÜL, Ph.D.

Professor of Architectural History, Department of Art, University of California, Santa Barbara. He joined the Sardis Expedition in 1963 as its architect, acquiring special responsibility for the design, reconstruction and publication of the Roman gymnasium complex. The Marble Court stands once again thanks to the support of the Turkish government and the Sardis Expedition. Yegül's book, *The Gymnasium Complex and the Marble Court* (1986) is his major contribution to the Sardis publications. In addition, he has published many articles and book chapters on Roman architecture and on Roman baths. Currently he is preparing a new book, *Bathing and Baths in Classical Antiquity*.

A. THOMAS KRAABEL, Th.D.

Dean of the College, Professor in the Department of Religion and Philosophy, Luther College, Decorah, Iowa. Dean Kraabel began working with the Sardis Expedition in 1966 and continues with this association today. His central profesisonal interest in the history of Judaism in Late Antiquity was served by his involvement with the excavation, reconstruction and publication of the ancient synagogue and adjacent rooms in Sardis. Thus, his many publications on early Judaism are supported by reference to the information developed from excavated materials from Sardis. Of course, the Sardis synagogue and its contributions to knowledge are the central theme of many of his publications. Forthcoming is *The Synagogue and Its Setting*, coauthored with A. R. Seager, I. Rabinowitz and J. H. Kroll.

JANE AYER SCOTT

Executive Director, Head of Publications and Research, and General Editor for the Sardis report and monograph series for the Harvard-Cornell Sardis Expedition, Harvard University Art Museums, Cambridge, Massachusetts. Her association with the Sardis Expedition began in 1969 and has continued to the present with ever-increasing administrative and publications responsibilities. Her efforts created the exhibition, "Twenty-five Years of Discovery at Sardis." Its visit to the Oriental Institute Museum provided a reason for this symposium. Thanks to her untiring editorial efforts, the series of Sardis reports and monographs are appearing in print. She is the author of two forthcoming volumes of the series, *Oil Lamps from Sardis* and together with R. L. Vann, *Early Travelers' Accounts of Sardis and Unexcavated Buildings* . Also forthcoming is her chapter, "Byzantine Glazed Wares" for the Sardis report, *Pottery: Hellenistic through Islamic*. In addition, she has published several articles on Byzantine artifacts and medieval travelers at Sardis.

PREHISTORIC SARDIS: A SUMMARY AND FORECAST

David Gordon Mitten

Since its inception in 1958, the Archaeological Exploration of Sardis has encountered numerous traces of pre-Lydian occupation, both in the city area itself and in its vicinity, especially along the south shore of the Gygean Lake (Mermere Gölü), near the great tumulus cemetery of Bin Tepe, along the north side of the Hermus (Gediz) Valley (Hanfmann 1983). These fall into two categories: exploration of deeply buried occupation levels of the second half of the second millennium and early first millennium B.C. by deep soundings at the HOB/Lydian Trench sector in the northwestern part of the city site south of the modern highway and east of the Pactolus Valley, and a series of burial and habitation sites of the third millennium B.C. along the south shore of the Gygean lake, which have also revealed major Lydian, early Roman, and Byzantine/Islamic occupation phases (Fig. 2).

Sardis's strategic location, rich mineral resources, and fertile, well-watered agricultural lands (Hanfmann 1983) may already have attracted settled human habitation during the Neolithic millennia or even earlier. No certain remains this early have yet been encountered, however, either at Sardis itself or in its immediate vicinity along the south side of the Hermus Valley. Outwash from the tilted and faulted hills of unstable conglomerates that comprise the foothills of the Tmolus (Boz Dağ) Range have deeply buried early settlements, although systematic surveys, such as that undertaken by Dr. Recep Meriç and his colleagues from Dokuz Eylul University in Izmir, may yet reveal them. Tantalizing stray finds, such as ground stone celts, found when the Smyrna-Ankara railroad was built late in the 19th century (Hanfmann 1951) and a small human stone head, in style similar to heads of terracotta and stone statuettes from Çatal Hüyük and Hacılar in a private collection (Hanfmann 1983 and Hanfmann and Ramage 1978) have spurred speculation about the earliest Sardians. The earliest extensive occupation in the Sardis region to have been excavated under controlled circumstances lies along the south shore of the Gygean Lake, where wave action has eroded the margins of the Bin Tepe ridge, revealing traces of third and second millennium B.C. occupation at at least three locations.

Small-scale campaigns of test excavation, under the writer's supervision, investigated these sites in 1967, 1968, and 1969. The most extensively excavated site, Ahlatlı Tepeçik, about 1 kilometer west of Tekelioglu Köyü, discovered in 1966 by Muharrem Tagtekin of the Manisa Museum, was intensively sampled in 1967 and 1968 (Spier 1983). Several Early Bronze Age pithos inhumations were discovered, as well as a Cycladic-type cist grave of schist slabs, similar to ones discovered at Iasos in Caria. The mouths of the large handmade pithoi, closed by stone slabs and cobble packing, faced east. A single inhumation in flexed position lay in each pithos, head toward the mouth; in one instance, there were two skeletons. They were accompanied by simple grave goods: red ware wide-mouthed single "rivet" handle jugs, metal objects such as dagger, knife blades, and straight pins (Spier 1983; Waldbaum 1983), terra-cotta spindle whorls, and in one case a bar-shaped perforated stone pendant. Occasional black ware beaked juglets, with incised, white-filled ornament, occurred as well.

The pottery is of fairly simple shapes, similar to ones from Kum Tepe in the Troad (Sperling 1976) suggesting that these burials may have been deposited fairly early in the third millennium B.C., later than the extensive pithos cemeteries at Karatas-Semayük in Lycia excavated by M. Mellink of Bryn Mawr College. Large quantities of thick black ware burnished bowls, with flat bottoms and a variety of pierced and tubular lugs, were recovered in the surrounding fill; these are similar to ones from Troy I and II contexts and to Early Bronze I contexts at Beycesultan (Lloyd and Mellaart 1962). Large, elaborate, beaked pitchers of *Schnabelkanne* type and lidded, tripod-based jars are virtually absent.

A variety of flake and blade tools of various cherts and other silicate stones, many showing the "silica sheen" of sickle teeth, and two fragments of obsidian blades, as well as a few ground stone tools comprise a varied stone industry. Stray lead and silver objects have also turned up. A tiny chipped lunate tool of chalcedony (Hanfmann 1983) from a context of Lydian date may be a fugitive from an even earlier microlithic tradition of composite tools, perhaps flint-barbed harpoons used by hunter-gatherers along the lake, teeming then as now with fish, water fowl, and migratory birds: the campsites have yet to be located.

A second site, Eski Balıkhane ("The Old Fishery"), located ca. 2 kilometers east of the village of Tekelioğlu Köyü, features extensive mortar and rubble walls and foundations of Roman date. The landowner had built a house on the eastern margin by the time of our visit in 1984. Abundant sherds of Early Bronze Age date and flaked tools and *debitage* exposed by wave action along the shore and scattered over the fields that slope gently upward to the south indicate the presence of an important third millennium B.C. site.

With the landowner's permission, two small trenches were excavated in 1969. They revealed five pithos burials (Fig. 3), similar to those found at Ahlatı Tepeçik. Two of these contained one-handled jugs. The most important pithos burial, a lid on its side with mouth facing east (Figs. 3 and 4), contained the flexed skeleton of a man accompanied by three vessels, a copper alloy knife blade along one femur, a small silver pendant in the form of a ram perforated at the shoulder under the jawbone, and two gold earplugs of sheet gold over an interior of granular material, one on either side of the skull at approximately ear level. This "grave of three metals" (Fig. 4, herein; Spier 1983) demonstrates the advanced level of metallurgical proficiency that these Early Bronze Age people had reached by the mid-third millennium B.C. It seems possible that the earplugs (Fig. 5), similar to ones occurring widely throughout western and central Anatolia at this time in both gold and stone, may be the earliest instance yet recorded of the exploitation of Lydia's most famous mineral resource.

Further clarification of the nature, time range, and affinities of this settlement/cemetery with other sites in western and central Anatolia must wait for further excavation of the site. These and other small third and second millennium B.C. sites that remain to be discovered and investigated in the vicinity of the Gygean Lake should eventually furnish us with a chronological sequence for the cultural development of the Sardis region during the third and second millennia B.C. and perhaps much earlier as well.

A third site, Boyalı Tepe, farther east along the south shore of the lake, consisted of several partially eroded pithos burials exposed by wave action and which were found in 1967. These pithoi, with heavy horizontal ridges and no handles, contained (in one case) black ware spindle whorls and two carinated, handleless, red ware wheel-made flasks. The impression is one of burials of Middle or Late Bronze Age date, perhaps around the middle of the second millennium B.C. (Spier 1983).

What was easily accessible to excavators along the lake at a meter or less beneath the soil surface is at Sardis itself deeply buried under more than a dozen meters of water-laid overburden and debris from subsequent human occupation.

The deep soundings at HOB/Lydian trench, carried out by the late Gustavus F. Swift, Jr. (Fig. 6) in 1960, 1962, and 1966 (Spier 1983) and by Andrew Ramage in 1984 and 1985, have revealed a succession of occupation layers, alternating with lenses and layers of water-deposited sands and gravels, perhaps laid down by floods of the Pactolus stream when it flowed farther east than it does today. These occupation layers contained numerous fragments of black, gray, brown, buff, and some red wheel-made monochrome wares, including many fragments of thick-walled jars. These are associated consistently with small numbers of sherds from vessels painted in dark paint on a light ground, in motifs that show close connection with the sequence of Aegean painted wares of the Late Bronze Age (ca. LH III B.C., ca. 1300–1100 B.C.) through the Iron Age (Protogeometric and Geometric), and down through the 8th century B.C., when Lydian painted and monochrome wares become clearly recognizable.

Imports from both the Aegean area and the Anatolian coast, and local imitations, probably from a number of workshops, are represented. Their presence attests a steady, if at times intermittent, interchange between the Aegean and the western Anatolian hinterland during these centuries. Whether this involved trade, arrival of newcomers, both of these, or other factors, cannot yet be determined. Legends of Greeks visiting the Sardis region after the Trojan War come to mind.

At the bottom of the 1962 sounding, a small, coarse red ware carinated pithos was discovered, lying on its side, containing small fragments of burned human bone. This cremation burial resembles those found at Troy VI and others at Osmankayası, at Boğazköy, and elsewhere in central Anatolia. The presence of this burial at Sardis, adapting the centuries-old Anatolian tradition of jar burial to this new practice, may indicate that there was at least a village-sized community in this part of the Sardis site during the 13th or 12th century B.C. Early Iron Age tools excavated in securely datable contexts (Waldbaum 1983), a stone stamp seal (Spier 1983), and the articulated skeleton of a small equid (Spier 1983) are other important discoveries from these layers. The deep sounding of 1984 and 1985 initiated by A. Rourege and concluded by C. Swenberg (1984) and R. E. Moorey (1985), which was intended to control the results of these earlier soundings, produced essentially identical results. One surprise was a number of Early Bronze Age sherds, suggesting that an Early Bronze Age occupation layer exists somewhere nearby, probably deeply buried. Scattered fragments of red-karinated Hittite-type beaked jugs and a tubular-spouted jug have also turned up in the HOB/Lydian trench and PN sectors (Spier 1983).

What are the prospects for future additions to our knowledge of Sardis and its vicinity in pre-Lydian times? Further deep soundings, especially in the still virtually uninvestigated central and eastern parts of the city, combined with wider exposure of the deeply buried Late Bronze and Early Iron Age layers at Lydian Trench, would provide more extensive and more accurate information about the nature of society at Sardis during those centuries and how Lydian culture developed from it. Much remains to be done at the Early Bronze Age sites along the Gygean Lake. Continued surveys in the Gediz Valley and vicinity will produce settlement patterns for all periods of human occupation in this region. Eventually, excavation of a stratified site, such as the settlement mounds at Kılcanlar near the village of the same name, north of the lake and southeast of Gölmarmara, will produce a coherent, detailed basis for our knowledge of the archaeological sequence from the early third millennium through the Lydian period of the 7th and 6th centuries B.C. in this part of western Anatolia, thus providing what may not be completely attainable at Sardis itself (Gunter, in preparation). If all these approaches are pursued, the prospect for steady increase in our knowledge of prehistoric Sardis and its vicinity is bright indeed.

REFERENCES

Hanfmann, G. M. A.

1951   Prehistoric Sardis, in *Studies Presented to D. M. Robinson* I, ed. G. Mylonos. St. Louis.

1967   8th Campaign at Sardis. *BASOR* 186: 186.

1968   10th Campaign at Sardis. *BASOR* 191: 10.

1983   *Sardis from Prehistoric to Roman Times.* Cambridge, Mass.

Hanfmann, G. M. A. and N. Ramage

1978   *Sculpture from Sardis.* Sardis Report 2. Cambridge, Mass.

Lloyd, S. and J. Mellaart

1962   *Beycesultan* I. *The Chalcolithic and Early Bronze Age.* British Institute of Archaeology at Ankara.

Maddin, R., J. D. Muhly, and J. C. Waldbaum,

1983   Metallographic Analysis of an Early Iron Age Laminated Iron Tool. *Metalwork from Sardis: The Finds Through 1974.* Sardis Monograph 8. Cambridge, Mass.

Sperling, J. W.

1976   Kum Tepe in the Troad: Trial Examination, 1934. *Hesperia* 45: 305-64.

Spier, J.

1983   Prehistoric and Protohistoric Periods, in G. Hanfmann, *Sardis from Prehistoric to Roman Times.* Cambridge, Mass.

1983   Late Bronze and Early Iron Age in the City Area, in G. Hanfmann, *Sardis from Prehistoric to Roman Times.* Cambridge, Mass.

LYDIAN SARDIS

Andrew Ramage

Until the first seasons of the Harvard-Cornell Expedition, the actual city of Sardis was largely a historical fiction. True, there was a huge Hellenistic temple (Figs. 35 and 49) and ample inscriptional evidence that the Greek and Roman cities were nearby. Not only were two columns of the temple still standing, but several impressive piles of brick and concrete masonry gave witness to the presence of enormous Roman buildings on the plain or on the northern slopes of the acropolis; the most obvious remains on the citadel were also from the late Roman era.

All these had been noted by successive travelers from the 15th century on. The temple, which was perhaps the most alluring to the illustrators and the excavators, was finally cleared in a systematic way by a team led by Howard Crosby Butler of Princeton between 1910 and 1914. Butler also excavated more than 1,100 Lydian graves in groups of rock-cut tombs just across the Pactolus stream to the west of the temple and about half a mile to the south on the same side (Hanfmann and Waldbaum 1975). Most of them had been robbed— only two seem to have been quite undisturbed— but even so, a considerable quantity of Lydian artifacts was retrieved, including pottery, jewelry, gems, and metal utensils, along with a few imports to give some broad chronological boundaries.

Tombs and artifacts, but no community; it was the same story across the valley of the Hermus River five miles to the north of Sardis. In the royal cemetery of Bin Tepe, or One Thousand Mounds, the enormous earthen tumuli of the kings of Lydia and Sardis had been celebrated since the time of the poet Hipponax and the historian Herodotus, and gave witness to the resources of the

Lydian empire (Fig. 8). The burial chamber in the middle of the biggest mound, that of King Alyattes (the father of Croesus), had been explored in the 19th century by Spiegelthal, the Prussian consul-general at Smyrna (Butler 1922). Our investigations confirmed that some of the chamber was made of finely tooled marble with elegant drafted edges. The excavations of the Harvard-Cornell expedition in the mound of King Gyges did not find the burial chamber, but they did reveal a substantial encircling wall of trimmed limestone within the structure, of which more than 150 feet were exposed.

Still there was no living community in evidence; the kings at Sardis had presumably ordered the erection of these huge markers, but nothing was showing of their legendary splendor in life. Almost all the elements that went to make up the picture of the capital of the Lydian Empire were owed to Herodotus and fragmentary allusions by other authors.

One may wonder what led Professor Hanfmann to dig at Sardis. Part of the answer may be a chain of unfinished business stretching from the outbreak of the First World War to the death of Professor George Henry Chase, Hanfmann's predecessor at Harvard. Chase had joined Butler's expedition in 1914 and had been assigned the publication of the Lydian pottery (Hanfmann 1972). In 1938 he invited Hanfmann to collaborate with him, a suggestion that eventually led to the formation of the Harvard-Cornell expedition.

Even with all the attention and study, a picture of Lydian Sardis has been slow to emerge. In particular, we lack the Sardis celebrated by historian and poet—the glittering Sardis of Croesus and Alyattes. One might say it is still emerging, and every recent season has added evidence of the physical grandeur that had been expected.

How should we characterize Lydian Sardis? I have taken the phrase to mean the period from the accession of Gyges and foundation of the Mermnad dynasty in the early 7th century, to the death of Croesus, following the fall of Sardis to Cyrus the Great of Persia in 547 B.C. This is arbitrary. Clearly the Sardis of Gyges was not created overnight, nor was it obliterated in the Persian conquest. On the contrary, we can see signs of very active city life and quickening connections with the Greek world well before the traditional accession of Gyges in about 680 B.C. Herodotus describes how looting by Persian troops was stopped in the moment of triumph, and the city subsequently became the prime administrative center of the Persian Empire in the west.

What we must do, then, to obtain the fullest picture we can is to combine the archaeological testimony with the literary—confirming, adding, and perhaps contradicting. This final possibility—of contradiction—is the most dangerous and a measure of last resort. It is, furthermore, most likely to be resisted by historians, because until recently they have had only to balance the written sources in order to reconstruct a probable course of events. Of course, archaeological "facts" are often susceptible of more than one interpretation; where possible, a combination of historical and archaeological is the most desirable. Time and again, outright denial of written testimonials, however absurd on the face, has proved hasty. On the other hand, uncritical acceptance of all written details in a literal manner can lead to an impasse. Through the excavation of the Lydian levels at Sardis, we have had a superb opportunity to expand the historical and cultural understanding of western Anatolia in the early historic period, which is also vital for a proper reading of early Greek history.

Clearly, our reports must describe the remains of Lydian Sardis we have found: buildings, potsherds, metalwork, ornaments, and all the equipment of a living community. We must set them in their sequence and explain their nature. But there is a greater responsibility— to coordinate them with a familiar picture of human actions that has been passed down from early times to the present.

Although there is a long record of earlier habitation and literary references to personalities of previous eras, Sardis can be seen to have emerged from the Dark Ages by about 725 B.C. This horizon is marked by widespread destruction in the Lydian Trench of the House of Bronzes excavation sector, an area that was excavated for nine seasons by the late G. F. Swift, Jr., one-time Curator of the Oriental Institute Museum (Fig. 7, No. 4). It is characterized by several clumps of building debris and stumps of walls, together with much broken and burned pottery in patches of ash. In addition, there were numerous skeletons left unburied and human bones gathered together in a pit (Fig. 10). There seems to have been a hostile action in that so many were not given funeral rites and many more were stashed together in a makeshift pit. A child of about eight was one of the victims; perhaps she was asphyxiated under a fallen roof.

That Sardis was a flourishing and outward-looking community at this time can be seen by the variety of imported pottery from this small group of structures. We can see pieces from Corinth, Rhodes, and Euboea, as well as many other anonymous "East Greek" or "Cycladic" imports, and Lydian pieces in imitation of them, among the traditional Lydian styles of pottery. An equivalent level in terms of the pottery mix and the type of building was found beside the Pactolus stream (Fig. 7, No. 13) at a distance of about half a mile, but the exposure was very small and there was no sign of wholesale burning such as that in the Lydian Trench. It does, however, illustrate the possibility that there may have been several small centers that eventually coalesced to form the city of Sardis as we imagine it. Pottery from this early period has turned up at several places around the site, but as yet the limits of early habitation in the area of the later city are unknown.

The destruction observed in the Lydian Trench does not correspond to any recorded event at Sardis, as far as we can tell, but it is more or less close to a number of events here and elsewhere. For example the violent destruction at Gordion, the capital of the Phrygian Empire some 250 miles to the east, is sometimes set about 700 B.C. and attributed to invading Cimmerians. The Cimmerians are supposed to have attacked Sardis several times during the reign of Gyges, according to Herodotus, and on one occasion sacked the lower town.

It is odd that there is no mention of any struggle in connection with Gyges' overthrow of Kandaules, the last of the Heraklid kings, even though there are hints in the literary sources of a long tradition of opposition among prominent families. Is this destruction the work of the Cimmerians, a little earlier than we thought? Is it the result of an internal struggle for power that was suppressed by Herodotus or his sources in favor of the story of Kandaules and Gyges for the sake of the anecdote or the moral? In either case, the account of our principal source needs to be adjusted, and it is hardly preferable to suggest an additional undocumented assault by the Cimmerians. Here is a genuine crux, where the combined efforts of archaeologists and historians might provide a resolution. Our finds have been reported over the years and duly noted by scholars, but I think they have not yet been appreciated in their totality for the impact they might have on the study of the Cimmerian invasions and the history of Sardis and early Ionia.

The city recovered from this blow, and at some undetermined time around the middle of the 7th century was rebuilt in roughly the same area. There is something new now in terms of planning. Whereas the simple buildings of the 8th century had shared a general orientation and were self-contained, the new buildings form a much more organized complex; they are either attached or in very close association (Fig. 9). Their wall construction is technically similar but much more substantial than before, and the architectural remains are much better preserved.

Not much remained, however, of the inhabitants' possessions, except for large quantities of local pottery. The general lack of imports compared to the abundance in the previous level is noteworthy, and suggests that trade relations (to the west especially) may have been made more difficult by the marauding Cimmerians, even though the community seems more prosperous. While the buildings may have been lived in and have many appropriate features such as hearths and storage facilities, we do not think that was their exclusive function. We suggest that they were also used for manufacture and trade; the linking of the units within a perimeter wall may be an attempt to control access to the "bazaar."

Most of these buildings were overtaken by flooding in the late 7th century, and many of them were covered by a thick layer of gravel or sand. Not long afterward occupation resumed and several small detached units were constructed. Much more of the occupants' personal property and equipment has survived from this level, most of which seems to date to the earliest part of the 6th century.

We find an increasing quantity of high-quality imported Greek ceramics and a growing number of Lydian imitations of them. This corresponds very well with the indication, from the historical sources mentioned in our introduction, of the purposeful hellenization of Sardis by the kings Alyattes and Croesus. The purple headscarves of Lydia, celebrated by the poetess Sappho of Lesbos, offered the Greeks something besides plain gold, and might have been woven in some of the small buildings in this area, to judge from the large concentrations of loomweights we have found over the years. Several pieces of stone moulds (Fig. 20) for casting jewelry—rings, plaques, or earrings—might have supplied the local or the export trade in jewelry. Another activity in the area was the fabrication of bone artifacts, especially straight pins with decorated heads, very like some that were found in the precinct of the temple of Artemis at Ephesus. These things in themselves may not be very valuable or exciting, but they are the material residue of the brilliant life of the high society of Lydian times and a concrete demonstration of its cosmopolitan character.

About 300 yards to the west of the Lydian Trench, and beside the river, is the excavation sector Pactolus North (Fig. 7, No. 10). Closely set domestic remains dating from the late 7th century to the 3rd have been exposed here. The most prosperous era in terms of finds, especially fine imported pottery, is in the first half of the 6th century. The spaces appear to be more tightly filled than in the Lydian Trench area, and there is the possibility of a public structure equivalent to a Greek fountain house, in the form of two apsidal areas, each with a well at its apex.

In another part of this area, to the north, there are remains of a gold-refining installation which operated from the late 7th century into the mid-6th. Set in the middle of the gold refining complex is a sacrificial altar made of roughly trimmed fieldstones, which was crowned by sculptured crouching lions at the corners. The lions show that the altar was dedicated to the goddess Cybele; a potsherd found close by, inscribed KUVAV, her Lydian name, confirms it. We found the lions immured with some of the debris from the sacrifices. The structure had been filled in and added to in a rebuilding, which we take to be a result of the Persian conquest and their dislike of animal sacrifice. An inscription that had been built into a Late Roman house about 400 meters upstream (Fig. 7, No. 42) attests to this directly, in that Persian priests are specifically enjoined from consorting with devotees of gods receiving burnt offerings (Hanfmann 1983).

This complex can be considered one of the most important discoveries of the expedition for connecting the picture of the Lydian Sardis of historians and numismatists with the physical remains from the trench. As always, it answers some questions but generates others, equally tantalizing. The reality of Lydian gold was never in doubt, and its legendary quantity was accepted, if not quite at face value. Our finds bring a new dimension to the picture of the wealth of Croesus and to the workshop practices of the time. We now know where and how goldsmithing was done from the remains themselves as well as from scattered notices among literary texts. We now have more than imagination to give us a picture of the workmen squatting by ash-lined hollows in the ground, pumping bellows into red-hot charcoal and melting the raw gold into little cakelike ingots (Fig. 12).

The "golden-flowing" Pactolus, which ran through the city, was celebrated in antiquity as the principal source of the gold, and we have learned that there was gold in many nearby streams. This raw gold would in fact be a natural alloy, with a substantial but variable fraction of silver (ca. 25 percent is common), or what the ancients called electrum.

At this stage we should remember two statements connected with the disposition of Croesus' wealth. One is a long description in Herodotus (I.50) of his gifts to Apollo at Delphi, which included 117 gold bricks and a gold statue of a lion. What concerns us here is that there were two kinds of brick, evidently signifying different qualities or fineness of gold. One kind, in greater quantity (113 bricks), was referred to as white, the other (four bricks) as refined; the lion, too, was referred to as refined, and weighed more than 500 pounds. The other statement (I.94) maintains that the Lydians were the first to mint coins in both gold and silver. (Title page illustration; silver coin of Croesus).

The interest of both these statements lies in the contemporary realization of the importance of having pure gold and pure silver. This is a technological event of the first order, and relates to the other features of the installation, which seem to be exactly suited for the parting of silver and gold by the traditional method of "cementation" described by the Italian master craftsman Vanoccio Biringuccio in his metallurgical handbook of 1540. This requires the hammering of the little ingots into thin sheets that are put in a pot in layers with a mixture of brick dust and salt. The whole thing is then kept at a red heat for a considerable time while the salt combines with the silver and leaves the gold pure. This can be repeated several times to increase the purity, and the sheets can be melted again into cakes. The actual evidence takes the form of many small pieces of thick gold foil, many pieces of wide-necked water pots which could have contained them, and two banks of simple square furnaces turned red by heat. Analysis of the residues shows substantial levels of silver, too, which is easily lost through the action of time and groundwater. We are confident that these installations were fully capable of carrying out the process Biringuccio described.

The altar of Cybele in the middle of this smokey industrial complex is something of a puzzle. I suggest that the goddess Cybele was associated with the extraction and manipulation of metals from the earth at Sardis, just as a great goddess (later combined with the Greek Aphrodite) was associated with metalworking at Bronze Age Kition in Cyprus (Karageorghis 1976).

The altar was constructed after the beginning of metallurgical operations because it stands at a higher level than some layers containing goldworking debris and because its core is composed of disintegrated brick of the type used for the furnaces and perhaps for filling the cementation pots. Unless there were an altar precisely beneath the present one, there was apparently no specific requirement for an altar on the premises and its presence must be explained in some other way.

Could it be that the altar represents a thank offering to the goddess for a technical breakthrough? This would have been the invention of the means to part gold and silver on a large scale. This kind of interpretation obviously goes beyond the limits of the evidence, but it brings us face to face with the results of a process that attracted notice from the ancient writers and can be seen in the progression of the Lydian coinage, from electrum to extremely fine gold or silver.

Lydian structures in the eastern part of Sardis are represented by the complex known as the Byzantine Fort (Fig. 7, No. 23), which is really a monumental platform at the end of one of the fingerlike spurs of the acropolis. The platform itself was composed of boulders and large pieces of dark rock from Mount Tmolus put together without mortar (Fig. 14). This was then faced with neatly cut limestone blocks trimmed in the typical Lydian fashion. We know that the width of the platform at the end of the spur was about 85 feet because we have located both corners. The length is as yet undetermined but the same kind of construction on a similar alignment has been found more than 60 yards away to the south. Yet another stretch of similar limestone masonry was found in the 1986 season about 100 yards farther on. These stretches of wall show every sign, in construction and siting, of having been part of a unified and continuous scheme to create a platform for a grand building and to enhance the grandeur of the slopes behind it.

Within these limits there are many traces of earlier remains from the 7th century on, including pieces of elegant multicolored stone bowls and an ivory handle in the form of a lion. As yet we are not sure of the purpose of the structure, which was apparently given these fine limestone walls during the 6th century. The palace of Croesus has been proposed, and should not be ruled out, but we cannot yet be certain.

This great terracing system is well up on the slope, but the sources indicate that there must have been at least a refuge on top of the acropolis. Some of this probably survives in the form of finely cut and tooled terracing walls on the north slope (Fig. 7, No. 20.2). These were made partly of white limestone and partly of greenish-yellow sandstone. Much of the top surface of the acropolis has eroded away, and continued building and occupation has almost eliminated the Lydian traces, except for a few objects such as the bronze boar mentioned in the chapter by N. H. Ramage (Fig. 21). There are a few stumps of rough-cut masonry remaining on the south side, which serve as additional reminders of the triple fortification circuit that so impressed Alexander the Great. Some of this circuit must have lasted into Roman times, since the Byzantine wall we now see is composed in part of white limestone blocks trimmed in the Lydian fashion, as well as miscellaneous marble architectural pieces from the Roman period. The heights of Sardis mentioned in an admiring way by the Greek poet Alcman must have been a splendid sight for the approaching traveler and a forbidding prospect for would-be invaders.

If the heights were girdled with a stone wall, the city itself seems to have had defensive works at some points, although Butler could discover no traces. Recently we have found that a series of mounds extending from the Roman gymnasium area (Fig. 7, No. 1) toward the east and into the plain contains remains of a stone structure that may form part of important buildings near the limit of the lower town. Only one face was exposed, but its alignment, which has shaped that of the hillocks, and an abrupt drop of about 20 feet to the plain at the north (exactly where the late Roman city wall now stands) give us every reason to suppose that there is an enormous Lydian building complex of unknown purpose forming the core of this huge pile of debris.

A trial excavation was made in 1985 and a run of more than 30 feet of cut limestone blocks was confirmed. It consisted of at least seven courses, making an exposed vertical face of about 10 feet and a substantial amount assumed below that. The square-cut white limestone face was surmounted by several courses of roughly trimmed dark grey stone. It was not clear whether this was a small-scale repair or an unusual inversion of the usual technique of finely cut stone over rough-cut stone. Evidence of destruction by fire was overwhelming and large quantities of mud brick, cindered and deformed by intense heat, were recovered.

Besides the structure itself, there is little associated material to give much of a date or context other than Lydian. Finds from the surface in the area of the face go back as far as the 7th century B.C., but as yet we cannot say whether this has anything to do with the original building of the structure or is just fortuitous. The finds do indicate, however, that the main life of the structure was in the 6th century B.C., so that this segment of masonry contributes directly to our understanding of the limits of the Lydian city. One supposition is that the city expanded a great deal in the late 7th and early 6th centuries under King Alyattes, and required a much bigger circuit than before.

This might explain the apparently odd situation of an enormous mud brick structure (Fig. 7, No. 63) about 100 yards to the east of the Lydian Trench, which appears to be the remains of a defensive wall but also seems to be in the middle of the city. Not only are there the extensive remains of occupation in the Lydian Trench, described previously, but also there are the remains of several houses or workshops directly in front of the east face of the wall and covered by the fall of debris from the superstructure. One of the rooms was full of kitchen vessels and utensils, as well as some barley and peas (Greenewalt et al. 1987). It also included two elegant, painted Athenian cups from the middle of the 6th century (one is described in the chapter on the arts at Sardis; Figs. 17 and 23), precisely the time when a defensive wall would have been needed. A nearby area may have served as a glassworking establishment, and another was certainly used for grinding and cooking meal in one way or another.

The preserved remains of unbaked mud brick rise on the east side about 25 feet from the stone socle, which was 60 feet thick. To judge from the fall of debris in front, it may have risen another 15 feet above that, although the upper parts may have been less substantial. This superstructure was quite probably composed of bricks in shades of green and red: unbaked green clay combined with the terra-cotta of fired bricks. The green bricks were also found in the face of the wall, on occasion laid with brown mortar for an additional colorful pattern.

It is unclear how the west side worked. It may have been a platform behind the higher curtain wall at the east but it has suffered from erosion and later interference. The building was not made exclusively of brick, however, because there is a substantial stone tower made of large, roughly trimmed stones attached to the brick face (Fig. 15). By any standards this is a remarkable scale of building and reminds us of the contemporary walls of Babylon and again of the legendary power of the Lydian Empire.

The picture we are building up of Lydian Sardis depends very much on developing a feel for the urban plan and the architectural features that form a setting for the daily life of the people. Except for the special details of the gold installations that are so important to the legend of Sardis, we have concentrated on presenting these larger elements without itemizing or describing those objects that must have furnished or decorated them. That side of the picture still needs to be filled in, for the monumental pieces of architecture have very few associated artifacts, and many of the finest artifacts have very little context.

We continue to look for more of Lydian Sardis by opening new trenches or reevaluating old finds. We want to find out how a village or clusters of dwellings grew into a city, what its buildings looked like, and what they were used for. We should also like to get a more precise idea of Lydia's relationship to her neighbors east and west, and more evidence for the chronology of Lydian styles. In spite of the success of our work and the descriptions of Herodotus, Lydian Sardis is still a tantalizing puzzle, but its magnificent existence is beyond doubt.

REFERENCES

Biringuccio, V.
  1540   *Pirotechnia*
            Translated with an introduction and notes by C. S. Smith and M. T. Gnudi 1942. 1966 in Boston, Mass.
Butler, H. C.
  1922   *Sardis I, The Excavations Part I, 1910-1914.* Leyden.
Greenewalt, C. H., Jr., N. D. Cahill, and M. Rautmann
  1987   The Sardis Campaign of 1984, *BASOR.* Forthcoming.
Hanfmann, G. M. A.
  1972   *Letters from Sardis.* Cambridge, Mass.
  1983   *Sardis from Prehistoric to Roman Times.* Cambridge, Mass.
_____ and J. C. Waldbaum
  1975   *A Survey of Sardis and the Major Monuments Outside the City Walls.* Sardis Report 1. Cambridge, Mass.
Herodotus
            The Histories.
            Translated by A. de Selincourt. Penguin Classics 1954. Baltimore.
Karageorghis, V.
  1976   *View from the Bronze Age: Mycenaean and Phoenician Discoveries at Kition.* New York.

LYDIA AND SARDIS IN ANATOLIAN CONTEXT

Machteld J. Mellink

Sardis and the Lydians who made it their capital form a major component of Anatolian Iron Age history and culture. The land of the Lydians, extending along the fertile Hermus Valley, had relatively easy access to the Aegean coast as well as to the Anatolian plateau, and its rulers established relations with their neighbors on both sides, west and east, while building a cultural and political entity for Lydia.

One of the questions concerning the formation of Lydia relates to its roots in prehistory. Most cultures in Anatolia are stratified and learned from their predecessors, whose physical elements they also absorbed. The Lydians did not start in a vacuum. The excavators of Sardis have contributed considerable evidence of the Bronze Age development of the greater Sardis area. Along the shores of the Gygean Lake, north of the Lydian tumulus cemetery of Bin Tepe, several sites of the Early Bronze Age were discovered and tombs of the mid-third millennium excavated. These cist and jar burials are of typical western Anatolian, so-called Yortan type, in layout and burial ritual. Tradition as well as some prosperity are already beginning to appear. One tomb at Eski Balıkhane had three kinds of metals among its burial gifts: a copper dagger, a silver ram pendant, and a pair of gold earstuds (Fig. 4). This is above average for the Yortan milieu.

The silver ram calls for artistic as well as functional analysis: Was it locally made? Were such small pendants worn as jewelry in Early Bronze Age Lydia? The people of these early settlements were in touch with customs and technology of western and central Anatolia in a modest way, and may have been developing their own metallurgy. We do not yet know where the major center of the area was, the Early Bronze Age predecessor of Sardis, and we need to find out about the architecture of this era. Some sherds of the third millennium B.C. turn up in the city site of Sardis, which therefore had some of the early occupation we are looking for (Greenewalt 1984, p. 369).

In the second millennium B.C., settlements continued to exist in the area of the Gygean Lake (Meriç 1985). Late Bronze Age sherds came from the deep sounding in the area west of the Pactolus (Hanfmann 1983). This period is of particular importance for the historical development of Lydia. We know that the Lydian language, as spoken and written in the era of the Iron Age kingdom of Lydia, is of second millennium derivation in Anatolia, perhaps related to Hittite. Was it the language of any of the kingdoms we know from Hittite records to have existed in western Anatolia during the Hittite Empire, and was the Hermus Valley proto-Lydian territory linguistically? These questions will remain prominent in future explorations of early Sardis and its vicinity.

One of the major monuments west of Sardis is the Hittite rock-cut image of a seated goddess on the northeast slope of the Sipylos mountain east of Manisa (Akurgal-Hirmer 1961); this inscribed relief and the rock reliefs at Karabel, some 30 kilometers to the south of Manisa, are direct links with Luvian and Hittite presence in the lands of the West.

The oral history of Lydia does not reach as far back as these monuments. It stops at the Dark Ages, which separate the Lydians from Hittite history. The names of the pre-Heraklid and Heraklid dynasts given by Herodotus (I.7) are a mixture of mythology and local reminiscence, ending with King Kandaules, also called Myrsilos, in Lydian (Maeonian?) and Hittite designation. The change to the Mermnad dynasty starting with Gyges is told by Herodotus in one of his first romanticized tales. The story of the ring of Gyges, narrated by Plato (Republic 2, 359 c-e; Pedley 1972), is another sample of the free style of Lydian history-telling by the Greeks. Herodotus knew of Gyges' connection with the Delphic oracle and of his dedications of gold and silver at the sanctuary (I.13–14).

Gyges, however, is better anchored in Assyrian as well as Egyptian history and chronology (Pedley 1972). With the rule of this king (ca. 685–645 B.C.) we can begin to correlate the Lydian historical tradition with archaeological evidence from Sardis, and consider whether the cosmopolitan contacts of the early Lydian rulers influenced and stimulated their building programs in the capital. What the form of the dynastic seat had been in the Dark Ages will have to emerge from future excavations at Sardis. For the period from the first to the last king of the Mermnad dynasty, through the rule of kings Gyges, Ardys, Sadyattes, Alyattes, and Croesus to the conquest of Sardis and Lydia by Cyrus of Persia in 547 B.C., the historian and excavator can work together to reconstruct the most glorious era of Lydia and its capital, which became a coveted prize to the Persians and ultimately a center of Persian administration, diplomacy and cultural inspiration in the West (Fig. 1).

The golden era of the Lydian kingdom was achieved through symbiosis with its neighbors: Ionians, Carians, and Phrygians. The Lydian kings, with some Assyrian aid, succeeded in defeating one of the major disruptive forces of the Iron Age, the Cimmerian horsemen who had ruined Midas of Phrygia and looted Gordion at the beginning of the 7th century B.C. Cimmerian hordes repeatedly threatened and invaded Lydia until Alyattes established control of the Lydian realm, which he extended to the Halys River.

Lydia indeed was a link between Greeks and the Orient, and became such a good neighbor of the Ionian Greeks (in spite of struggles to obtain control of coasts and harbors) that the Lydian land was imbued with East Greek culture, to the extent that it often becomes impossible for us to tell East Greek and Lydian traits apart. On the East side, Lydian proximity to the Phrygians and their gradually established control of the Phrygian culture resulted in mutual borrowings in material, if not linguistic, culture. Here the excavators of Gordion have a task to share with those of Sardis in analyzing the vicissitudes of these two major centers of western Anatolia and their interaction from ca. 700 B.C. to the Persian conquest.

Both Phrygians and Lydians were in contact with the rulers of Mesopotamia; Midas with Sargon of Assyria, Gyges and his son Ardys with Assurbanipal, Croesus with Nabonidus of Babylon. Egypt was also within the foreign horizon of the Lydian kings, from the days of Gyges' assistance to Psammetichus I of the Saite dynasty to Croesus' alliance with Amasis. This Egyptian contact, established with the aid of Ionian and Carian ships and crews, added to the foreign cultural potential of Lydia beyond that of its Phrygian neighbors and predecessors.

The historical background briefly sketched shows the great promise for the present and future excavations at Sardis. The work is taking place in a capital of the ancient world, a successor of ambitious centers and dynasties founded by Hittites, Luvians, and Phrygians in central and western Anatolia, and a seat of kings who had the wisdom and strength to merge old and new in their own land with the best they could draw on through contacts with Mesopotamia and Egypt. They made peace and shared cultural enterprises with the Ionian Greeks, who were also extending their ambitions overseas and reconciling Bronze Age heritage with Iron Age innovations. The failure of Lydia against the pressure of newcomers in the Near East was postponed by an alliance of Alyattes and the Medes in 585 B.C., when the Halys was agreed upon as the boundary between greater Lydia and the kingdom of Kyaxares. The capture of Sardis by Cyrus and his Persians in 547 B.C. was to some extent a case of *Lydia capta ferum victorem cepit*, as is evident from the prominent role of Sardis in the history and culture of the Persian Empire and other empires subsequently.

What have the excavations of Sardis so far revealed of the material and cultural evidence of the dynasty from Gyges to Croesus? In reviewing the main achievements it should be kept in mind that we are reversing the order of excavation to reconstruct the chronological development, and that we can expect proportionately less substantial revelations as the trenches deepen and narrow.

The nature of Sardis as the site of the Lydian capital differs in a fundamental respect from that of Phrygian Gordion. The citadel of Sardis is not built on a stratified mound consisting of the accumulations of centuries of building, demolition, replanning, destruction, and rebuilding. Rather, it is set on a mountain spur dominating the Hermus plain by its natural elevation and strategic position. In this respect Sardis can be compared even to the citadel of the Hittite capital at Hattusha, which was selected for its strategic advantages at a late stage of prehistory, shortly before 2000 B.C. The citadel of Hattusha was fortified separately almost from its beginning, while the lower city was protected by its own enclosure walls and grew with extensions to the higher and lower ground south and north, with additional systems of ramparts and gates. We are beginning to see that Sardis was a similar major strategic center, controlling the road through the Hermus Valley with the establishment of a watchpost and stronghold on the acropolis, and expanding its lower city with a system of protective enclosures and terraces descending from the northern slopes of the acropolis.

As all visitors to Sardis know, the citadel has suffered through natural erosion and landslides as well as Byzantine reoccupation. What has been emerging of the Lydian citadel is both impressive and surprising in its monumentality: terraces with ashlar retaining walls, the masonry with its drafted edges of excellent quality (Hanfmann 1983), connected by stairs. David Stronach and Carl Nylander, in their studies of early Achaemenid masonry at Pasargadae, referred to these acropolis terraces at Sardis as the likely sources of technical and formal inspiration (Hanfmann 1983). New discoveries in progress in the northeastern part of the lower city are exposing more of an ashlar-faced terrace wall (Fig. 14) along the spur of the "Byzantine Fort" (C. H. Greenewalt 1985, 1986), which now, as it follows the spur and curves with it along its eastern side, begins to look like a line of fortification rather than a separate platform in the lower Lydian city of Sardis. Another such terrace wall came to light on the north side of the lower city in 1985 (Greenewalt 1986). The possibility that this northern segment belongs to an extensive fortification system of the lower Lydian city is to be considered.

The date of the beginning of such Lydian masonry has not yet been established. The Byzantine Fort terrace or rampart seems to be post-560 B.C., but it shows a mature style and technique. The excellence of Lydian masonry was developed in contact with stone workers of the Ionian world and presumably initially inspired by observation of Egyptian monuments and workmanship. The outcome is masonry of Lydian character, which will reveal its chronological development as the excavators disentangle the monumental articulation of the lower city of Sardis.

Excellent masonry has also been found in the tomb chambers of the tumuli in the great Bin Tepe cemetery (Fig. 8) north of the Hermus River. The possibility that the large tumulus nicknamed Karnıyarık Tepe is the tumulus of Gyges would raise exciting hopes for early Lydian architecture and history. The chamber is still elusive; tunneling along old robbers' passages revealed an interior retaining wall of coursed ashlar blocks crowned with a round molding. Large monograms on the upper course, tentatively read as Gugu, suggest the identification (Hanfmann 1983). The tumulus of Alyattes, anciently plundered and often disturbed, with its marble chamber, gives a safer date for the introduction of fine marble masonry and surface finishes in the context of the early 6th century (Hanfmann 1983).

The spectacular tumuli of Bin Tepe belong to the kings and noblemen among the Lydians of Sardis. We may someday know the qualifying criteria for this type of burial, which was introduced into Anatolia in the Iron Age. Phrygian aristocracy was buried in tumuli from at least the 8th century B.C. on, as attested by the excavations at Gordion. Phrygian burial chambers are built of timber and have no doorways. They are descendants of timber-lined, covered burial pits, resembling kurgan burials in southern Russia and Scythian burials, which have wooden burial chambers covered by piles of rubble and large earth mounds. Lydian tumuli, as known so far from Sardis and elsewhere, invariably have stone chambers constructed with doorways and sometimes anterooms and short dromoi; the burial chamber is therefore symbolically and practically provided with access. The relationship of these chambers to the Phrygian series, which starts in the Iron Age several generations before Gyges, is unmistakable but not yet clear in all details. The Lydians either modified the Phrygian concept (which had become grandiose in the case of Midas, whose giant tumulus covered a large, gabled wooden chamber protected by an outer timber casing, a rubble pile, and a stone retaining wall) on their own or combined it with the Aegean notion of chamber tomb burial, which western Anatolia adopted in Mycenaean times, and may be the inspiration of the chamber tomb series in the west cemetery at Sardis.

With respect both to the ideas that shaped the Lydian tumulus burial and to the study of the format of the built stone chambers in the tumuli, their contents, and decoration (to which wall paintings also may belong), it is to be hoped that the exploration of Bin Tepe, difficult and demanding as it may be, will continue to be part of the digging program. The tomb chambers, with few if any exceptions, will have been looted in the past, but excavation and analysis will be able to retrieve much of the basic evidence.

The Bin Tepe tumuli were set at a considerable distance from the city and citadel across the Hermus River, visible on the northern horizon with identifiable giant landmarks such as the mounds of "Gyges" and Alyattes. Other tombs of more modest format were cut or built to the west of the city across the Pactolus, or even on its east bank. The so-called Pyramid Tomb (Hanfmann 1983) stood on what must have been the outer slopes of the lower city, outside of the rampart, as a separate monument of an important person. To the west, the first Sardis expedition excavated over 1,000 chamber tombs, rockcut with dromos and doorway, dating from the 7th century on (Hanfmann 1983), and made Lydian pottery and jewelry known through its discoveries. All of these tombs were extramural, outside of the walled lower city area and mostly grouped in cemeteries, as were the Bin Tepe tumuli.

The lower city of Lydian Sardis, long elusive under the monumental overburden of Byzantine and Roman structures, has finally begun to emerge in the course of the last decade of digging. The start was the identification of the truncated hillock south of the modern road as the stump of a huge mudbrick fortification, the tracing and analysis of which is still in progress. The details of the course of this rampart, its vicissitudes from its original construction through war, destruction, and rebuilding, and the continuation of the wall from a point southeast of the synagogue along the spur pointing to the acropolis, are coming to light in spite of intensive Roman intrusion into the remains of the "monumental mudbrick structure."

This discovery is most gratifying. We now can put Sardis in the series of great cities of Iron Age Anatolia and the Near East, protected by ramparts, towers, and gates. Herodotus, our loyal guide through much of Ionian, Lydian, and Persian history, is ambiguous in his statements on the topography of the lower city of Sardis. When Cyrus in 547 B.C. made his surprise raid to reach Sardis in the west, he had followed the Phrygian road from Pteria, the site of the undecided battle between his and Croesus' forces, and had taken Gordion, which was protected by a garrison under Lydian auspices. At Gordion, Cyrus found the main citadel rebuilt with stone walls and gates, protecting the megara and official buildings of the Phrygian-Lydian administration and noblemen. A suburb along the east side was separately fortified with a mudbrick rampart 12 meters high constructed of 120 courses of mudbrick, with towers and gateways along its east face. The Persian troops besieged this outer city and succeeded in scaling the wall with the aid of a ramp; heavy fighting took place and arrows flew back and forth. Many arrowheads were found stuck in the mud plaster of the outer face of the rampart; the barracks, which stood to six meters height on top of the mudbrick rampart, were attacked and burnt (Young 1957; Edwards 1959). This was the end of Lydian control of Phrygia; a Persian governor and garrison took over command from the Lydian contingent at Gordion.

The troops of Cyrus continued to the Hermus Valley and reached Sardis, where evidently an equally formidable mudbrick rampart prevented their entry into the lower city. The attack must have been carried out with tactics similar to those at Gordion. As the excavations of recent years have exposed the built and rebuilt mudbrick wall protecting the lower city of Sardis at the northwest side, they have revealed a structure some seven meters high of solid mudbrick on a masonry base. This structure suffered sudden damage to its superstructure from a conflagration in what must be the year 547 B.C. A large piece of burnt mudbrick debris toppled onto a house full of Lydian inventory neatly dated by imported Attic cups (Fig. 13; N. Ramage 1986), providing a remarkably precise sample of archaeological history retrival and correction of Herodotus' simplified account of what happened when Cyrus reached Sardis.

It will be left to the excavators to sort out the history of the great mudbrick rampart, which seems to have been built by Alyattes. It may have been besieged, as was the mudbrick fortification at Gordion, with the aid of a ramp. This device is commonly used in military sieges of the era and were applied to the attack of Old Smyrna by the Lydians themselves under Alyattes ca. 600 B.C. The core of this Lydian-built siege mound survives at the northwest corner of the mound at Bayraklı (Cook and Nicholls 1958–1959). At Gordion, the outer mudbrick rampart was demolished after the Persian conquest, but the ramp was left as a visible monument. The main citadel with its stone fortification walls became the Persian center of command. At Sardis, the stone wall which was built on top of the stump of the mudbrick wall, presumably a functional repair, may have been commissioned by the Persians themselves. It was attacked by the Ionians in 499 B.C. Herodotus (V.100-102) reports that the lower city or outskirts of Sardis caught fire because of the reed huts and thatched roofs of mudbrick buildings, and that the conflagration extended to the temple of Kubebe.

Most of this disaster could have taken place outside of the walled area, where Kubebe's sanctuary probably was located. Here again the topography of the Herodotean account will be clarified by the Sardis excavations. The ruins of the temple of Kubebe have not yet come to light. The archaic model of a Kubebe shrine (Hanfmann and Ramage 1978), a three-dimensional naiskos, shows the Ionic-Phrygian affinities of the Lydian cult figure and her entourage. The standing goddess has been Ionicized in attire. Neither the Phrygians nor the Lydians have so far yielded native iconography of the goddess Kybele-Kubebe; in

Phrygia she borrows her image from Kubaba of Neo-Hittite and Carchemish tradition; in Lydia, the Phrygian adaptation of the Neo-Hittite image is put through the process of Ionic transformation. We can expect more light on the Lydian career of this goddess and her sanctuary in Sardis.

Marble sculpture from the excavations at Sardis does not provide a general clarification of the nature and originality of Lydian art and imagery. The Greek traits prevail over the Lydian. It may be different in terracotta. Andrew Ramage has studied the polychrome architectural revetments of Sardis, which have also been put on such vivid display in a sample replica of roof tiles and friezes in the excavator's compound (Ramage 1978). The early use of architectural terracottas, before the arrival of Cyrus, is made probable by the new analysis. Both Alyattes and Croesus knew of such colorful ornaments. The designs are a blend of orientalizing, Greek, and Lydian inspirations. Among the puzzling designs of the revetments is that of the old fragment showing Theseus in combat with the Minotaur (Åkerström 1966). This is surely archaic, and it would be important to know if this type existed in Sardis before the Persian conquest. We do not have a complete version of this scene from Sardis in full painted detail. It surely would have looked more accomplished than the painted version of this subject on revetment plaques from Gordion (Åkerström 1966), which in unpainted state appear surprisingly Ionic in the facial features of Theseus. What this scene meant in the context of ca. 525 B.C. in Lydia or Phrygia under Persian rule, or ca. 550 B.C. in the days of independence, can be presumed by comparison with the hero-killing-monster scenes which become so prominent in Achaemenid iconography. In these a horned lion takes the place of the bull-man. The scene at Sardis and Gordion is derived from the Greek tradition, however. It had come to Phrygia because the Lydians had adopted it, along with other Lydianized versions of Greek ornament and iconography, all of which in essence contained oriental inspiration. The complex syncretism of Ionic, Lydian, Phrygian, and basic oriental art and iconography is typical of 6th century greater Lydia; the story of Theseus and the Minotaur may have had less impact than its illustration glorifying the local royal hero vanquishing a monster.

If we finally have a look at the pottery of Sardis, which after all forms the bulk of the material in the excavators' storerooms and study rooms, the cosmopolitan nature of Lydian arts and crafts becomes more and more evident. It is most vivid in the still growing collection of fine and domestic pottery from the house crushed in 547 B.C. (N. Ramage 1986). Lydian pottery proves itself of fine quality, with its judicious use of dark, even, or streaked, banded or undulating, glaze. Shapes have two sources. They may be basic western Anatolian, with a shared Phrygian component. Pitchers, jugs, dishes, storage pots, are all reliable shapes of second millennium ancestry or a somewhat modified imitation of Greek (skyphoi, lekythoi, amphorae, kraters). The one shape that appropriately received its name from its makers, the Lydion (Greenewalt 1967, 1978), is an exception.   This handleless, conical-based ointment vessel (Fig. 13) was widely used inside and outside of Lydia.   The Lydians introduced this shape into the world of ceramic containers and perfumed-ointment trade.   They may have found inspiration for the shape from alabaster vessels that came from Egypt.   The Lydion was thoroughly studied by the director of the Sardis excavations while he was still engaged in studying the Phrygians.

However this may be, and wherever we focus on aspects of Lydian art and artifacts, the culture of the Lydians, in all its splendor and maturity as developed under their own kings from Gyges to Croesus, is becoming much better understood and appreciated through the annual campaigns at the great site of Sardis.   The understanding radiates to the west and east, to Ionia and Greece as well as to Phrygia and Persia, and it has a deep foundation in Anatolia itself, as the Bronze Age levels of Sardis and the study of the language and religion of Lydia increasingly reveal.

We must be thankful for the great initiative of George Hanfmann in reopening the excavations of Sardis and to his splendid team of colleagues and successors who are so well represented in this symposium.   George Hanfmann was proud of his team, and Sardis is lastingly proud of him.

REFERENCES

Åkerström, A.
    1966   *Die architektonischen Terrakotten Kleinasiens.*   Acta Instituti
                Atheniensis Regni sueciae, Series in 4°, XI. Lund.
Akurgal, E. and M. Hirmer
    1961   *Die Kunst der hethiter.*   Munich.
Cook, J. M. and R. V. Nicholls
    1958–1959 The Lydian Capture of Smyrna.   *BSA* 53 and 54: 23–25 and
                128– 34.
Edwards, G. R.
    1959   The Gordion Campaign of 1958.   *AJA* 63: 263-68.

Greenewalt, C. H., Jr.

1967   *Lydian Pottery of the Sixth Century B.C.: The Lydion and Marbled Ware.* Ann Arbor. University Microfilms, Inc.

1978   Lydian Elements in the Material Culture of Sardis. *Proceedings of the Xth International Congress of Classical Archaeology.* 37–45. Ankara.

1984   Sardis: Archaeological Research in 1983. *VI Kazı sonuçları Toplantısı.* 367–77. Izmir.

1985   Sardis: Archaeological Research in 1984. *VIII kazı Sonuçları Toplantısı.* 299–310. Ankara.

1986   Sardis: Archaeological Research in 1985. *IX kazı Sonuçları Toplantısı.* Ankara. Forthcoming.

Hanfmann, G. M. A.

1983   *Sardis from Prehistoric to Roman Times: Results of the Archaeological Exploration of Sardis 1958–1975.* Cambridge, Mass.

Hanfmann, G. M. A. and N. H. Ramage

1978   *Sculpture from Sardis: The Finds through 1975 .* Sardis Report 2. Cambridge, Mass.

Meriç, R.

1985   1984 yilli Izmir ve Manisa illeri yuzey arastirmalari   *III Arastırma Sonuçları Toplantısı.* Ankara.

Pedley, J. G.

1972   *Ancient Literary Sources on Sardis .* Archaeological Exploration of Sardis. Cambridge, Mass.

Ramage, A.

1978   *Lydian Houses and Architectural Terracottas.* Sardis Monograph 5. Cambridge, Mass.

Ramage, N. H.

1986   Two New Attic Cups and the Siege of Sardis. *AJA* 90: 419–24.

Young, R. S.

1957   Gordion 1956: Preliminary Report. *AJA* 61: 319–31.

THE ARTS AT SARDIS

Nancy H. Ramage

When we say "the arts at Sardis," we are talking about objects made by the Lydians themselves and about those produced by the Greeks, the Romans, the Persians, the barbarians, and others. All were found at the site, and most, but not all, were of local manufacture. Sardis was a cosmopolitan place, and an urban center. Because of the city's position between the Greeks to the west and the Anatolians and Persians and other orientals to the east, not to speak of passing barbarian hordes, there were many opportunities for foreign-made objects to find their way to Sardis. Keen trade was one of the hallmarks of Lydian life, and the people were very interested in the luxury products of their neighbors. The citizenry was subjected to many influences, and sometimes the artists produced objects that were strongly reminiscent of what one finds at other places in the vicinity, or at cities with which Sardis had trade or other contact. Yet, objects made at Sardis also have characteristics which are local and recognizable. As we discuss the works in question, we shall look for characteristics which reflect other nearby peoples and for those which seem to have a special Lydian stamp to them.

One might well ask, Why would anyone try to review the art produced at a particular site over the whole course of antiquity? Or shall we say, from early Greek times to late Roman? After all, there were many places near Sardis where such an effort would not make much sense. For instance, at Pergamon, the importance of the place only blossomed in the Hellenistic period, after the time of Alexander the Great. In other places, such as Smyrna, the center of the city changed substantially from one side of a huge bay to another, and thus digging in one place produces remains only of certain eras, and one must go elsewhere to find any continuity. At Sardis, on the other hand, the thread of creativity seems to transcend the rule of particular dynasties or political powers, and thus the production of artists is carried on for over a millennium within a relatively limited area.

We shall examine some of the most interesting and attractive of the thousands of finds from Sardis which might be categorized as "art," keeping in mind, though, that many of them were created for practical uses. Just as sculpture was often made for the purpose of making dedications to the gods, so ornaments were used for personal adornment, and objects such as pottery or horse trappings, which we now study as artistic products, were used in daily life.

One of the most characteristic items produced in the archaic period of Lydia was stone lions. There are many examples which survive, and one can only surmise how many more once stood in Sardis and the cities nearby. Lydian lions, usually crouching, are akin to Greek lions, but are if anything more compact and more stylized than their western counterparts. The ferocity of the beast is not emphasized so much as the smooth, elegant outline of body, mane, and tail.

Lions were symbols of Lydia's most important goddess, Cybele. It is thus no wonder that they show up on sculptural reliefs associated with her. Sometimes they flank her throne, and sometimes she holds a lion in her arms. On one particularly interesting piece of sculpture (Fig. 16), Cybele is flanked by snakes— another of her attributes— and may have been carrying a lion in her arms. Other lions are relegated to reliefs on the side, depicted as if decorations on the walls of a shrine; and the goddess is shown as if in her temple, which must have been Ionic, to judge by the preserved bases for the columns. Other reliefs on the side include dancers and priestesses who are portrayed as if moving forward to make offerings to the goddess. The reliefs on the back of the block portray mythological scenes, including one showing Herakles fighting the Nemean lion. This sculptural work is a treasure house of information on the worship of Cybele, on the development of shrines in the 6th century, and on local iconography. It is thus remarkably fortunate that the piece was reused as a building block in the synagogue, where it was found wedged in the middle of a supporting pier.

This so-called Cybele shrine was one of a number of dedications to the goddess, and we know that the making of offerings to the gods was universally practiced in the ancient world. Among the most famous of these dedications, reported by the Greek historian Herodotus (I.50), were the offerings which Croesus made to Apollo and the oracle at Delphi. They consisted of a lion made of gold and weighing nearly 570 pounds; two cauldrons, one of gold and one of silver; other vessels of gold and silver; a golden statue of a woman, said to represent the baker of Croesus' bread; and much jewelry which belonged to his wife. Herodotus emphasizes the wealth of the king, and he revels in details, especially those showing how expensive were the materials dedicated by Croesus. This is one of our most descriptive references to the fabled wealth of the king.

We also know that Croesus paid for the carving of the Ionic columns of the temple of Artemis at Ephesus. Most unusual was a series of maidens who marched in shallow relief around the column shafts. Fragments of this sculptural decoration, preserved in the British Museum, give us an idea of how intriguing it would have been to have a forest of columns decorated with these archaic women, who remind us of the servants carved on the sides of the Cybele monument from Sardis.

One has to turn to a foreign work to see any representations of Croesus himself. On a Greek pot in the Louvre, the painter Myson portrayed him at the quintessential moment, when he was about to be burned on a pyre by his vanquisher, the Persian king Cyrus (Hanfmann 1983). Then, suddenly, on the appeal of Croesus, Apollo took pity on him and sent a burst of rain to put out the already-lit fire. The story, which has a moral tone to it, relates that Croesus finally understood the message of the great Athenian Solon, who had said that "no man should be called happy until he was dead" (Herodotus I.87).

A domestic and industrial area from the time of Croesus was remarkably well preserved by the fallen debris from the fortification which stood next to it. In the attack by Cyrus and his armies, a part of the huge structure fell right on top of some rooms, and sealed and preserved their contents in an undisturbed state. Among the many finds from these floors were four pieces of fine pottery from the mainland of Greece: two from Corinth and two from Athens. It is the latter two which we use to date the floors to the period of the great battle between Croesus and Cyrus, since both of them can be placed just before the middle of the 6th century B.C., when the battle is dated by independent historical sources. One of them was a so-called komast cup, which showed a pair of lively dancers (called komasts) on each side. The other (Fig. 17) was a drinking cup with beautifully painted spotted panthers decorating the band between the handles. Although restored from many pieces, the cup displays a variant of the very elegant shape of the deep "skyphos" which was particularly favored by the Lydians.

We have seen how Croesus was portrayed by a Greek artist. If one wants to see how the Lydians portrayed their own, one has to turn to a work such as the delightful fragment of an architectural terracotta with the profile view of a head of a man, which was cut down from a much larger piece (Fig. 25; A. Ramage 1978). He has large eyes, a pointy nose, and a neatly trimmed beard, but is clean-shaven around the jaws. His long hair falls behind the ears, revealing a prominent earring. We call him the "Lydian Dandy," following an old Greek saying. It is interesting to note that the only worked object in gold to turn up near the refinery described above was a small earring decorated with a recumbent lamb (Fig. 19). It suggests in a tantalizing way what other marvelous jewelry of this type must have been lost, although a fair amount was found and published by the first Sardis excavation (Curtis 1925).

Not only the jewelry itself but also molds and dies for casting such pieces as earrings (Fig. 20) and gold foil decorations were found at Sardis. One of the most beautiful is a square die, made of copper alloy, that is decorated with numerous delicate patterns, including circles and bead-and-reel (Waldbaum 1983). Another ornamental piece (Fig. 18), carved in bone, is a roundel with designs on it that reveal workmanship of the nomadic tribes. They were regarded as barbarians by the Greeks and surely by the Lydians too. This piece, which is one of four such examples so far identified from Sardis, shows a bird or griffin wrapped around itself in a design which is well suited to the round shape of the object. It may have been dropped behind when the Cimmerians, who seem to have been a tribe related to the Scythians, raided Sardis in the 7th century B.C.

Two particularly interesting metal decorations, portraying an ibex and a boar (Figs. 21 and 22), were each probably intended for a horse's harness. The ibex, or mountain goat, was a favorite motif in the eastern Mediterranean. The fact that the piece is unfinished argues for local manufacture. The boar, which was found on the acropolis, may be another example of Lydian workmanship (Waldbaum 1983). Boars were often depicted in this part of the world, which is not surprising, considering that the animal is still frequently spotted and hunted in the mountains. In fact, one of the guards at Sardis recently had a young boar as a pet, which was much admired by the staff and workmen until he began to attack certain people he did not like!

On an imported cup from Athens, found on the acropolis, we again find this animal, but this time in a mythological scene of "the Calydonian boar hunt" (Fig. 23). The tale tells of the hero Meleager and his female helper, Atalanta, who kill the wild animal that had been sent by Artemis to ravage the land. We see here the hunters spearing the boar, which is being attacked also by a white dog on his back. This painting is found on a "merrythought cup," named for its wish-bone handles; an inscription near the rim encourages the reader to "drink and be merry." It is one of the finest cups of its type, and bears testimony to the very high quality of the objects that were being imported to Sardis from mainland Greece in the first half of the 6th century.

In fact, the Lydians had been importing pottery from Greece for a long time. During the late 8th and the 7th centuries, the international market had been dominated by the workshops at Corinth, and Sardis was no exception to the many sites around the Mediterranean that found their pottery appealing. The animal and ornamental floral styles of Corinth were in some ways akin to the East Greek pottery of Rhodes and many other places along the western littoral of Asia Minor, and their designs rubbed off on local Sardian pot painters. Crawford Greenewalt has identified certain characteristics of the Sardis style, which can be seen, for instance, in a deep open vessel (Fig. 24) decorated with friezes of animals, including spotted deer and roaring lions with their tongues hanging out; empty spaces between them are taken up by filling ornament (Greenewalt 1970). The vigorous and lively style and the vivid red and brown paint on a white background are local characteristics, and make this a particularly attractive piece.

A Sardian pot painter decorated a small cup with a pair of fish, placed head to head, on each side. It was found in a small grave west of the Pactolus stream and behind the massive hills of the necropolis. Again, dotted ornaments fill the empty spaces, and a double row of rays pointing up from the base, and the shape itself, remind us of the influence of Corinth (Greenewalt 1972).

In the second half of the 6th century, and in the 5th and most of the 4th, Sardis was under Persian rule The artistic production, naturally enough, reflects a Lydo-Persian conflation of styles which is especially evident in sculpture and gems. One example of this can be seen in a sculptural relief depicting a funeral meal (Fig. 26), where the gentleman reclines on a couch while his wife sits beside him on a stool. A servant, holding a flower in her hand, stands behind. The theme was favored by the Persians and is here taken up by a local sculptor who was also clearly aware of mainland Greek conventions. We can see this particularly in the three-quarter position of the wife. The piece reminds us of the many seated women on Greek funerary monuments. A similar theme is found on the marble pediment of a small mausoleum, the remains of which were found in the Pactolus stream bed. This relief has the funeral meal, but here, more figures, including perhaps other family members and servants, are represented. The heavy wear on this piece by centuries of flowing water do not obscure the sculptor's awareness, again, of both Persian and Greek elements (Hanfmann and Erhart 1981).

The worship of Cybele did not diminish in this age, but she is sometimes joined by her kindred goddess Artemis (Fig. 27). In a large votive relief, each of the two frontal goddesses holds an attribute: Cybele a lion and Artemis a deer, representing the latter's role as protectress of the hunt (Hanfmann and Ramage 1978). This time, two small worshippers, who stand admiringly in profile at the sides, emphasize the monumentality of the goddesses. Above their heads hangs a tambourine, another common attribute of Cybele. The relief is important in that it proves that the two goddesses, often thought to have been worshiped as one at Sardis, also kept their distinct and individual identities.

In this period, Lydian gem cutters were heavily influenced by their Persian counterparts, who were great masters at the trade. Small though these objects are, they are among our very important sources for observing the meshing of cultures in the Lydian capital. On one example, found far from Sardis on the Black Sea, a gem can be proven to be of Lydian manufacture because of the Lydian inscription on it. The figural design, typical of Persian art, shows two crowned royal sphinxes facing each other in a heraldic pose (Boardman 1972, Fig. 834). They remind us of the beautiful gold applique ornaments found in the Princeton excavations early in this century; again, two crowned and winged sphinxes face each other, this time beneath a winged solar disk (Curtis 1925). The tiny holes around the edge would have allowed these thin gold objects to be sewn onto fabric.

On another gem, found in Lydia, a man in Persian costume attacks a lion (Boardman 1972, Fig. 844). Of course it is difficult to tell whether these objects were cut by a Persian or a Lydian artist, since Sardis was one of the satrapal capitals of the Persian Empire, and we know there were many Persians living there. But it is clear that Sardis was heavily under the influence of these foreigners, and yet she did not reject her contacts with the Greeks either. Another gem from this period, found at Sardis, portrays Hermes and Athena in a completely Greek manner (Boardman 1972, Fig. 855). In objects of such a personal nature as tiny gems, one wonders if Lydians had a preference for one style or another, or whether they simply chose subjects which appealed to them, regardless of the artistic origin.

After Alexander the Great swept through Asia Minor, Anatolia, and on toward India, the Persian influence at Sardis disappeared, for when Alexander defeated the Persian king Darius at the great battle of Issus, Persia lost her empire in the west. Sardis became a more thoroughly hellenized city, although keeping something of its local character. One of the most important buildings from this period preserved at Sardis is the great Hellenistic temple of Artemis. Not only can we study here the expert carving of the beautiful Ionic capitals (some of which were replacements in the Roman period) but also, by good fortune, a fragment of a colossal cult statue to Zeus which survived the trials of time. This statue would have balanced a similar one to Artemis, of which no fragments have been found. From the head of Zeus, we have the beard and part of the cheeks, nostrils, moustache, and neck. Although not very prepossessing in its present state, the finely finished surfaces which are still to be seen in a few areas testify to the high quality workmanship which must have gone into this important statue. It is interesting to note that a Roman cult statue to the Emperor Antoninus Pius, to whom, together with his wife, the temple was later rededicated, is of almost exactly the same colossal dimensions.

One of the great events in Sardis was the devastating earthquake which seriously damaged the city in the year A.D. 17. In fact, the strong influence of the Greek world of the Hellenistic period seems to have continued more or less in an unbroken thread until that disaster, whereas the sculpture and other objects which may be assigned to subsequent periods have much more of a Roman stamp to them. It may be that with the infusion of funds from the Emperor Tiberius, who is known to have granted special aid for the rebuilding of Sardis, the local people had a new respect and sense of gratitude toward the Roman capital.

One of the great civic projects at Sardis was in fact erected to bring honor to one of the Roman emperors and his family: the early 3rd century grand hall attached to the bath-gymnasium complex, about which there will be more detail below. For now, we concentrate on the the engaging sculpture which decorated the capitals on the colonnade at the entrance to the so-called Marble Court. Each of these capitals was adorned on both ends with the head of a mythical figure, which either looked in toward the Marble Court itself or out toward the exercise ground in front of this complex. Zeus, Dionysus, Medusa, satyrs— these are some of the examples of the mythological figures whose heads peer out from among the leaves on the Corinthian capitals. One of the most intriguing is a helmeted male whose sharply turned head and thick muscular neck suggest a Hellenistic prototype (Fig. 28). He may be Ares, who is normally shown with a helmet such as this. The deep-set and intense eyes and the attention to bony and muscular details of the face make this one of our finest pieces of architectural sculpture.

Roman painting at Sardis has survived mostly in tombs, many of which were cut into the rock below the peak of the acropolis, and along the bank of the Pactolus. Two of the better preserved of these were decorated with the peacock, symbol of eternal life. One, named after this image, is the so-called Peacock Tomb and the other, called after its owner, is the Tomb of Chrysanthios (Fig. 47). Doves, wreaths, baskets of fruit, and flowers strewn everywhere added to the gay effect of the latter's walls. Another remarkably well-preserved late Roman painting was preserved on the apse of a building built into the monumental Lydian fortification wall. Here, the decoration was abstract, with rectangular and circular panels painted so as to look like marble. They remind us of the well-known slope houses recently excavated and restored at Ephesus (Strocka 1977).

Another pictorial means of decoration common in the ancient Roman world was floor mosaic. In an elegant villa in the area of Pactolus North, several large segments of such mosaics were found, with delightful motifs of dolphins, birds, and animals (Hanfmann 1972). Each of these is set within geometric patterns which divide the large spaces into segments.

Many Romans, especially those of means, were buried with coffins decorated with traditional funereal symbolism or mythological scenes. Portraits of the dead were often added to make these monuments more personal. The best-known example from Sardis, and now in the Archaeological Museum in Istanbul, is the sarcophagus of Claudia Antonia Sabina (Morey 1924). She was a wealthy lady of the early 3rd century A.D., whose grave monument was placed along the main east-west road that ran more or less along the same route as the Izmir-Ankara highway that we use today. Full-length representations of her and another woman, presumably her daughter, show them reclining on the lid of the coffin, with a dog lying at the foot of the carved bed. Portraits of these aristocratic ladies show the fashionable hair-styles of the day. Although this piece was found by villagers and excavated by the Princeton excavation early in this century, it was not until the 1960s that an inscription was discovered showing that the same woman contributed funds for the building of the Marble Court.

Many fragments of another Roman sarcophagus turned up in the Pactolus stream bed. These would have made up another fine coffin like the one of Claudia Antonia Sabina, and although this one cannot be identified, the beauty of the modeling on some of the pieces attests to its high quality. One of the finest is the head of a horse which originally projected from the corner of the funeral bed portrayed on the coffin lid (Fig. 29). The artist gave a great deal of attention to the bone structure, texture of flesh and mane, and even to the expression of the horse; its flaring nostrils, open mouth, and twisted head give it much character.

Another female head from the same sarcophagus may be either an idealized portrait of a young woman or a type representing no one in particular. The piece might have belonged to one of the standing figures on the side of the coffin, filling the arches and pavillions which typically lined the so-called Asiatic sarcophagi. The beautiful head, which gazed downward, is draped with a mantle over the wavy hair and classicizing features.

A much greater attempt at realism is found in some of the Roman portraits found at Sardis. A magnificent head of an older man, bearded and with moustache and banks of wavy hair framing his face, was found lying face down in the bedding of a late Roman road (Fig. 30). It may have been knocked down from its position between the columns of a portico which lined an earlier roadway. The modeling of his cheeks and brows, and the sensitive deep-set eyes peering out from hairy eyebrows, give this man a remarkably wise and penetrating look. The artist was also very skilled at contrasting the textures of the deeply drilled hair of the beard and temples and forehead with the chiseled hair of moustache and eyebrows. This, together with the fine treatment of the wrinkles and flesh, combine to make him one of the best examples of Sardian sculpture from the Roman period.

Much cruder, but very effective in its bold carving, is a late Roman portrait which the staff at Sardis nicknamed "Sourpuss," due to the down-turned mouth and extraordinary expression on his face (Hanfmann and Ramage 1978). The over-life-size head is made to seem even larger by the frame of spiraling curls which lie low on the forehead. The face is almost abstracted into simplified shapes, a feature typical of late Roman sculpture. The head seems to gain a certain forcefulness and power from the rough style of the unknown artist. This piece was found near a lime kiln in the synagogue, and was undoubtedly destined to be thrown in to be burned for lime. We are fortunate that it was spared this fate, which undoubtedly befell countless pieces of ancient sculpture.

One of the most typical of late Roman objects is a small winged cupid or angel carved in bone (Fig. 31). Classical in concept, with long curls and topknot, naked body, and Roman features, he was made in a rather crude manner which betrays a lack of understanding or concern for the workings of the human body. Yet his slightly crooked stance and asymmetrical pose, with one arm across the body, and his charming expression make him into a lively and appealing sculptural work. He is one of those transitional pieces found all over the Roman world, straddling the traditions of classical antiquity and the craftsmanship and aims of artists working in the service of the early Christian church. It would not be long before images of cupid, symbol of love and son of the pagan goddess Venus, would be reincarnated as the Christian angel, with virtually no change other than the context.

This review of the arts at Sardis has allowed us to look at some of the more representative and outstanding examples of worked objects found at the site. We have seen that some were of local manufacture and others imported or left behind by foreigners. These objects reflect the artistic and political relationships which Sardis had with her neighbors in Asia Minor and Anatolia, and her contacts with more distant cities on the mainland of Greece, the peninsula of Italy, and as far east as Persia. They suggest the kind of composite picture of local talent and foreign influences that one finds in the remains of this cosmopolitan city.

REFERENCES

Boardman, J.
  1972   *Greek Gems and Finger Rings.* New York.

Curtis, C. D.
  1925   *Jewelry and Gold Work. Part 1: Seasons 1910–1914. Sardis XIII.*
            Rome.

Greenewalt, C. H., Jr.
  1970   Orientalizing Pottery from Sardis: The Wild Goat Style, *CSCA* 3:
            55–89.
  1972   Two Lydian Graves at Sardis, *CSCA* 5: 113–145.

Hanfmann, G. M. A.
  1969   On Late Roman and Early Byzantine Portraits from Sardis,
            Hommages à Marcel Renard, III. Collection Latomus. 103.
            Brussels.
  1972   *Letters from Sardis.* Cambridge, Mass.
  1975   *From Croesus to Constantine: The Cities of Western Asia Minor
            and Their Arts in Greek and Roman Times.* Ann Arbor.
  1983   *Sardis from Prehistoric to Roman Times.* Cambridge, Mass.

_____ and K. P. Erhart
  1981   Pedimental Reliefs from a Mausoleum of the Persian Era at
            Sardis: A funerary meal, *Studies in Ancient Egypt, the Aegean,
            and the Sudan: Essays in Honor of Dows Dunham on the Occasion
            of his Ninetieth Birthday.* Boston.

_____ and N. H. Ramage
  1978   *Sculpture from Sardis: The Finds through 1975.* Sardis Report 2.
            Cambridge, Mass.

Hirschland, N. L.
  1967   The Head Capitals of Sardis, *BSR* 35: 12–22.

Morey, C. R.
  1924   *Roman and Christian Sculpture. Part I: The Sarcophagus of
            Claudia Antonia Sabina.* Sardis V. Princeton.

Ramage, A.
  1978   *Lydian Houses and Architectural Terracottas.* Sardis Monograph
            5. Cambridge, Mass.

Ramage, N. H.
  1979   A Lydian Funerary Banquet, *AnatSt* 29: 91–95.
  1983   A Merrythought Cup from Sardis, *AJA* 87: 453–60.
  1986   Two New Attic Cups and the Siege of Sardis, *AJA* 90: 419–24.

Strocka, V. M.
  1977   *Die Wandmalerei der Hanghäuser in Ephesos,* Forschungen in
            Ephesos 8:1. Vienna.

Waldbaum, J. C.
  1983   *Metalwork from Sardis: The Finds through 1974.* Cambridge,
            Mass.

METALWORK AND METALWORKING AT SARDIS

Jane C. Waldbaum

The expression "rich as Croesus" is a familiar one. It has come to denote someone who enjoys the pleasures of limitless wealth and the power that often accompanies it. Few realize, however, that this expression is rooted in historical fact; that Croesus was a real king whose very real riches were based on an abundance of natural resources, particularly gold, with which his kingdom of Lydia and its capital Sardis were blessed.

Croesus of course is long gone, and his wealth has long since been dispersed, but the legends that have grown up around him since antiquity have attracted the interest of many to his capital—from treasure hunters in all ages to modern archaeologists who have ultimately explored many more aspects of the art and culture of ancient Sardis than simply the gold of Croesus. Nevertheless, the gold remains a lure, and beyond that, the metal industry and metal products of Sardis were in several periods of her history a source of prosperity and prestige, and therefore are worthy of our attention.

Over 1,000 metal objects found at Sardis have already been described in previous publications (Waldbaum 1983). These objects come from all phases of Sardis' history—Bronze Age, Lydian, Persian, Hellenistic, Roman, Byzantine, and Turkish—and include examples of all the metals known to have been utilized in antiquity: iron, copper and its alloys bronze and brass, silver, lead, and of course gold. These metals were used for a variety of purposes at ancient Sardis, just as they are now. Bronze, brass, and iron were used to make utilitarian objects of all kinds—tools and utensils for domestic and agricultural purposes, carpentry and masonry tools, nails and clamps, weapons and armor for the many battles fought in the history of Sardis, and shopkeepers' stock-in-trade: hardware, locks and keys, pots and pans. Gold, silver, and fine bronze were also used for more decorative and luxurious purposes—statues and statuettes, jewelry, mirrors, and cosmetic implements for the boudoirs of the ladies of Sardis, as well as for vessels and ornaments to be buried with the dead or dedicated to the gods, and for the liturgical equipment of the local pagan, Christian, and Jewish clergy. In addition, a number of finds in other materials such as stone molds and clay tuyères, or bellows nozzles, attest to the manufacture of metal objects in certain periods.

The study of the metalwork and metal industries at Sardis has taken many forms. Stylistic and typological study of the archaeological finds themselves has been combined with study of ancient literary sources, inscriptions, scientific analyses and investigations of the materials and workshops where metalworking was carried on. The analytical program was instituted in order to supplement information on the shape, function, and date of particular pieces with insight into how they were made and what their major alloying ingredients were. The information thus gathered is the result of collaboration among many specialists — archaeologists, epigraphers, geologists, metallurgists, analytical chemists, conservators, and others — all of whose determinations have been brought together to help form the picture of the use and importance of metals at Sardis through the ages.

Gold was the most famous of Sardis' mineral resources. Ancient authors tell us that the chief source was the alluvial gold washed down from Mount Tmolus by the Pactolus stream. According to Strabo (13.1.23; 13.4.5) native gold had been exploited at least from the time of Gyges in the 7th century B.C. through the time of Croesus in the mid-6th. But by Strabo's own time, toward the end of the 1st century B.C., the gold in the Pactolus had apparently been exhausted. Although the gold industry in the Lydian era is thus documented, it is not known exactly how long the gold supply lasted.

After the Persian conquest in 547 B.C. Sardis became a tributary of the Persian empire. A Persian source of the 5th century B.C. reports that Sardian gold was among the tribute brought to the capital at Susa, where it was worked by Median and Egyptian craftsmen. This tribute implies that Lydian gold sources were still productive at least through the end of the 6th century and possibly into the 5th. Hellenistic inscriptions from Sardis testify to rather lavish use of gold to ornament bronze portrait statues, a practice which the late George Hanfmann suggested might indicate the continued local production of gold (Waldbaum 1983).

The Lydians were noted for wealth in silver as well as gold, and as A. Ramage has already pointed out, the Pactolus gold was actually a natural electrum with a high silver content. Silver could be separated from the gold by the practice of cementation, described herein by A. Ramage. Other sources of silver, including silver-rich lead deposits, have been identified within easy range of Sardis.

The sources of the other metals used at Sardis—copper, iron, tin, zinc, and lead—have not yet been precisely identified, though most, with the exception of tin, were probably to be found in ore deposits that were fairly accessible to Sardis.

The history of metal production at Sardis begins in the Early Bronze Age with several objects found in or near the tombs at the Gygean Lake (see Mitten, herein, Fig. 4). Although the number of finds was not great, they already show use of at least three different metals (gold, silver, and copper) and a variety of functions—two decorative earplugs (Mitten, Fig. 5), three small copper daggers, three copper or copper alloy straight pins, a silver pendant in the shape of a ram, and three silver finials. The earplugs have been analyzed by neutron activation and shown to be made of gold with a silver content ranging from about 6 to 15 percent in different parts of the pieces. The varying composition is curious, since it has been assumed that each was made of a single piece of sheet metal. The high silver content, however, suggests that the Early Bronze Age inhabitants were already exploiting the natural electrum of the Pactolus. One of the daggers was also analyzed by optical emission spectrography and found to be made of a nearly pure copper rather than alloyed with tin to form bronze, while two of the pins proved to be alloyed with small amounts of arsenic. Recent analytical research on material from all over the Mediterranean shows that the use of pure copper or of copper alloyed with arsenic rather than tin is in fact the norm for this period.

Metal finds of the Middle and Late Bronze Age are exceedingly rare, and the next era for which we have clear evidence is the Lydian. Herodotus, the 5th century B.C. Greek historian, provides several anecdotes recounting the vast wealth dedicated by the Lydian kings to the sanctuary of Apollo at Delphi. Gyges, the first king of the Mermnad dynasty, who lived in the first half of the 7th century B.C., is reported to have dedicated several offerings of gold and silver (Herodotus I.14) including six golden bowls weighing a total of 30 talents (one talent weighs between 60 and 80 pounds). Alyattes, who reigned in the early 6th century B.C. also gave gifts to Delphi, including a silver vessel on a welded iron stand crafted by an East Greek artist, Glaukos of Chios (Herodotus I.25). The iron stand apparently remained in place long after the gold and silver had been removed and itself attracted the attention of later writers for the uniqueness of its craftsmanship.

Croesus, Alyattes' successor, gave even more. In addition to the famous lion monument described by A. Ramage herein, his gifts to Delphi included two large bowls—one of gold, one of silver. The gold bowl weighed over eight talents, and the silver had a capacity of over 5,000 gallons and was crafted by Theodoros of Samos, one of the most famous East Greek sculptors and metalsmiths of the Archaic era. (The employment of Glaukos of Chios by Alyattes and Theodoros of Samos by Croesus suggests the high value placed on Greek artisanry by the non-Greek Lydian kings.) Croesus also gave to Delphi a life-sized gold statue of a woman (honoring his baker who saved him from being poisoned) and numerous smaller objects of precious metals which Herodotus does not bother to describe in detail (Herodotus I.50, 51). In addition to what he lavished on Delphi, Croesus hedged his bets by dedicating valuables at other Greek shrines as well. He is said to have exactly duplicated his gifts to Delphi at the Milesian sanctuary of Didyma in western Turkey and to have donated golden bulls, sculpted column bases, and other rich offerings at the sanctuary of Artemis at Ephesus, which was closely linked to the cult of Artemis at Sardis itself (Herodotus I.92).

Needless to say, very little of this conspicuous wealth remains today. While many of the gifts of Croesus and his ancestors to Delphi were apparently still in place in Herodotus' time, nearly 100 years after the time of Croesus, practically none was to be seen there when the traveler Pausanias made his visit in the 2nd century A.D. By then, most had already been melted down or carried off. Sardis herself had been subject to continuous plundering, looting and grave robbing since at least the time of the Persian conquest, leaving only pitifully few Lydian objects in gold or silver and not much more in other metals to be found by the current expedition.

All traces of monumental sculpture and vessels in precious or other metals have vanished. Most of the evidence for metalworking in this period consists of small-scale objects, supplemented by the very important find of the gold refinery described by A. Ramage herein. One tantalizing small survivor of the age of Lydian glory is a tiny melon-shaped gold bead, now in the regional museum at Manisa, the segments of which are separated by rows of delicate granulation (Fig. 19). The bead owes its survival to its deposition in the protected environment of a grave dated to the second quarter of the 6th century B.C. In the same tomb was a small piece of gold wire attached to an agate bead. Both were analyzed by neutron activation and proved to be gold of a high degree of purity, possibly products of the refining activities which were being carried on contemporaneously. (It is interesting to note, in this regard, that the contemporary lamb earring, described by N. Ramage herein and shown in Fig. 19, contained a very high proportion of silver— over 30 percent— showing that it had been made of unrefined, or even diluted, electrum.) These were among the very few preserved objects in gold from all of Lydian Sardis.

Two examples of small-scale decorative relief sculpture from the 6th century B.C. are of bronze. They are flat plaques, one in the shape of a reclining boar, the other, a smaller one in the form of a recumbent ibex with head turned back over his rump. Judging from the attachment loops on the backs, these were probably used as horse trappings. (Boar: Fig. 21; N. Ramage herein; ibex: Fig. 22) The interesting thing about the ibex is that it is unfinished; the edges are unsmoothed and the surface lacks the sharp detail of a finished product. This almost surely indicates that the piece was being manufactured in Sardis and was discarded for some reason, perhaps because of casting flaws, before completion. Unfortunately, the context in which it was found does not shed any light on possible workshop practices, but the piece does provide valuable evidence for a local Sardian school of decorative bronzework that should probably include the boar as well. Parallels in ivory for both boar and ibex have been found in the sanctuary of Artemis at Ephesus, where we know the Lydian kings made gifts. Several close relatives to the ibex in bronze are also extant in a number of museum collections, though only the Sardis piece comes from an excavated context (Waldbaum 1983a).

Sardis was conquered by the Persians in 547 B.C., and traces of the battle have been preserved in the form of arrowheads of Persian types found on the acropolis and in the lower town (Fig. 11). Several of these have been analyzed by optical emission spectrography and/or atomic absorption, and most were shown to be tin bronzes to which lead had been added, presumably to increase the fluidity of the melted bronze during casting. Since arrowheads were more or less mass produced, and were intended to be expendable, perhaps the lead was also used to reduce the amounts of more expensive tin and copper in the alloy, and thereby cheapen the products. Similar types of arrowheads are known from many other sites in Anatolia and Greece, which came into conflict with the Persians in the 6th and 5th centuries B.C. Over 3,600 examples of a three-edged, socketed variety of arrowhead were found at the Persian capital of Persepolis itself. Although most of the Sardis arrowheads came from contexts that were not stratigraphically revealing, they and the parallels from Persepolis and elsewhere help to dramatize the violent events of 547 B.C. that caused the downfall of the wealthy Lydian kingdom (Waldbaum 1983).

Despite Sardis' position as a major Persian, Hellenistic, and Roman city, we know little of her metal industry for some centuries after the fall of the Lydians. Stratification of the later periods at the site is disrupted, and we have not chanced on much other than sporadic finds from these centuries. An area of industrial debris in a Hellenistic level of the House of Bronzes sector (Fig. 7, No. 4) may shed some light on bronze production in that era. According to an unpublished report by the late G. F. Swift, Jr., the industrial deposits here extended over an area some 8 to 10 meters in diameter and about 50 centimeters thick. They contained fragments of the clay floor of a furnace, pieces of clay molds, earth discolored by heat, fragments of charcoal and corroded copper and/or bronze, slag pieces, and quantities of animal bone (possibly to make bone ash for flux). All of this material perhaps suggests the presence of a bronze foundry. The full significance of this area and its associated finds has not yet been studied, nor has the exact type of industrial activity carried on there been determined. Large quantities of the materials from this industrial area have been stored in the laboratory at Sardis and await future scientific investigation.

The next era for which the evidence is more complete is the late Roman/early Byzantine, ca. 3rd through early 7th centuries A.D. Here we find a very different situation from that in the Lydian era. It appears, indeed, that in the late Roman/early Byzantine era the foundation of the metal industry at Sardis was not gold, but iron and copper and the copper alloys bronze and brass, and that the objects for which Sardis was known at that time were not luxury items but functional and utilitarian products.

According to what we know from ancient sources, the Roman imperial metal industry in general was subject to a high degree of specialization. Different towns throughout the Roman Empire manufactured goods of special quality or distinctive types which were then dispersed by trade to other areas of the empire. One town near Sardis, for example, is known to have specialized in producing nails, another bed frames, and a third building materials, while Sardis herself was famous for production of iron-cutting tools—knives, rasps, swords and engraving tools (all of which presuppose the working of hardened steel to suit their special functions).

The peak of the Sardian iron industry came in late Roman times (3rd–4th centuries A.D.) when Sardis was the seat of an imperial weapons and shield factory or *fabrica*. Such factories, instituted under Diocletian, were very large and employed big work forces. They were operated by the state and were supplied with raw materials such as iron and charcoal by the state. Workers were ranked as soldiers and tied to their occupations by heredity. Such an institution would clearly have had an important effect on the social, economic, and political life of the community in which it operated. Since the factory at Sardis was one of only three such establishments in Asia Minor, it must have represented a substantial undertaking (Foss 1976).

The factory buildings at Sardis have not been located or excavated, and surprisingly few weapons attributable to the late Roman period have been found on the site. Clive Foss suggests unexcavated Building A (Fig. 7, No. 24)—a large 3rd to 4th century A.D. building in the center of town—as a possible location for the factory (Foss 1976), but there is no evidence to support this identification. In fact, the central location of Building A among the public structures of Sardis argues more strongly against its housing a large, noisy, and smelly industrial establishment. In 1979 a detailed surface survey located an area of industrial activity with a heavy concentration of slag and late Roman coarse pottery on the surface of the ground near the northeast edge of the late antique city wall (Fig. 7, No. 9.15). This area may have some relation to the *fabrica*, which further exploration would reveal. A few objects from the same period have been tentatively identified as smith's tools (Waldbaum 1983, nos. 143–148), although none can be associated specifically with the *fabrica*. Several inscriptions, however, confirm the existence of the *fabrica*.

The most interesting of these inscriptions were discovered in 1976. They are painted inside the 4th century A.D. tomb of a well-to-do man announcing the dedication of the tomb to its owner, "Flavios Chrysanthios, *ducenarius* and worker in the arms factory." Another inscription in the same tomb says that the owner was both *ducenarius* (apparently his official title) and painter of images (*zoographos*), and furnished or decorated his own tomb (Greenewalt 1978; see N. Ramage herein for description of the tomb). The term *ducenarius* here is interpreted by epigraphers as connoting a high-salaried official who may have been director of the arms factory (though there is some question about this). His amateur interest in painting is unusual for someone of his presumed social rank, and this discovery may give us evidence for one of the first "Sunday painters" in history.

The arms factory was a major industry, turning out weapons for the troops of Rome. Manufacture of items for local consumption took place on a smaller and more local scale. And for this we have considerable evidence both for the products and for their production.

The great bulk of the metal objects that we have found date to the early Byzantine era (6th to early 7th centuries A.D.) and come from two areas located fairly close together at the site. These were the "House of Bronzes" on the south side of the modern (and ancient) highway (Fig. 7, No. 4) and the Byzantine shops on the north side of the highway, just across the road from the house (Fig. 7, No. 3). Judging from the many liturgical objects with Christian symbolism on them found in the house, it probably belonged to a Christian cleric (some have suggested the Bishop of Sardis) of the late 6th to early 7th centuries A.D. The metal objects from the House of Bronzes were all found together on the floors of a basement storeroom, where they had been left when the house was burned and abandoned. The Byzantine shops form a kind of shopping center near the main part of town. They are arranged in two long rows of some 25 to 30 small shops set on either side of the main colonnaded street through town. One row, backing onto the great late Roman gymnasium and synagogue, has been excavated. The shops and the House of Bronzes were destroyed simultaneously in the early 7th century A.D. by an invasion of Sassanian Persians, leaving many of their contents intact and *in situ* and providing us with a great deal of valuable, well-dated information.

The shops themselves were small and narrow, one- or two-room cubicles with their wares stacked both inside and outside on the sidewalk within the colonnade. One can picture them when busy as closely resembling a modern

Middle Eastern bazaar. Objects found in the shops probably constituted most of the individual owners' stock-in-trade, together with equipment such as steelyards and balances for weighing out goods. Various household items such as copper pots, pans, jugs, and bowls were probably made or finished on the spot and then piled on the floor and outside the door to attract customers, again anticipating modern practice.

One of the shops has been nicknamed by the excavators "the hardware shop" because it contained quantities of tools, utensils, and odds and ends of the types that would be sold in any hardware shop from then to now. Like many hardware dealers, the shop owner was also a locksmith, for among his wares were nearly 200 bronze and iron locks in various shapes and sizes — some not yet finished, but either in process of manufacture or repair (Fig. 52). Most of the locks were heavily corroded, but some had their mechanisms at least partly preserved, giving us some clue to the action of these locks. Most were made of a front and back plate with a keyhole on each side and the bolts and springs sandwiched in between. Keys were also found, though curiously most of the keys recovered were not of a type that would correspond to the majority of lock types found. Most of the keys were small and probably fitted the locks of small ornamental caskets or boxes. They were frequently attached to rings that could be worn on the finger to prevent loss (rather like wearing mittens on a string around the neck).

Found in both the House of Bronzes and the Byzantine shops were a number of fine copper alloy vessels and Christian liturgical objects. The forms of those found in the house and the shops were similar, suggesting that the objects were made in the shops on one side of the road and put to use in the cleric's house on the other. Several incense burners or censers, for example, were found in both shops and house; some were round, some hexagonal, and some hemispherical, all with three little feet and three hanging chains attached to the rims (Fig. 54). In Byzantine ritual these censers would have been filled with glowing coals of incense and swung by the priest, who carried them in procession.

A related object from the House of Bronzes storeroom, and now in the Manisa Museum, is a fine incense shovel for lifting hot coals of incense. It has a flat, square scoop, a heavy four-armed cross at the back surmounted by an arch, and two stylized dolphins with lifted tails forming decorative side pieces. The surface of the cross is decorated with incised circles, and the markings on the dolphins are also incised. At the back is a hollow socket into which could be fitted a wooden handle for carrying it about (Fig. 55). Numerous parallels can be found elsewhere in the eastern Early Christian/Byzantine world.

The most interesting of the secular objects from the late Roman/early Byzantine period are the 29 buckles that were found. Eleven came from the

Byzantine shops, and the rest were scattered among such locations as the acropolis, the gymnasium complex, the synagogue, Pactolus North, and elsewhere (Waldbaum 1983). The buckles show a wide variety of forms (Fig. 53), but most can be shown to belong to groups of closely related types distributed widely throughout Europe and the Near East, and generally dated to the 6th and early 7th centuries (Fig. 53, left). Since many have been found in barbarian graves belonging to Bulgars, Avars, Lombards, and the like in Hungary, South Russia, Albania, Greece, Romania, and Italy, some scholars believe they were made by the barbarians themselves. Others suggest that they were made in a single center, such as Constantinople, and sold to the barbarian "market." Whatever the case, these objects were almost certainly imported into Sardis and may attest to the presence of some of those same barbarian invaders who ushered in the Dark Ages in Europe. A particularly handsome and unusual example, found in one of the Byzantine shops, is a large buckle hinged to a plate with double eagle heads at the corners (Fig. 53, center). The piece was cast and deep circles were punched on the surface, probably to hold inlays in contrasting materials such as glass or paste.

As with earlier material, scientific analyses were performed on a number of examples of Roman and early Byzantine metal objects. The results show that the alloys used were quite different from those used in earlier periods. For example, while most of the Lydian objects tested by emission spectrography or atomic absorption proved to be tin bronzes or tin bronzes to which some lead had been added, most of the early Byzantine cast copper alloys including many of the buckles and censers, as well as other objects such as lamp chains, lamp holders, and crosses, turned out to be rather curious quaternary, or four part, alloys containing not only tin and lead but also zinc in varying proportions. Hammered sheet metal objects such as vessels, on the other hand, were for the most part of nearly pure copper, while several Roman/early Byzantine cosmetic implements were true brasses, containing zinc but no significant amounts of tin or lead (Waldbaum 1983, Chap. V).

The occurrence of ternary and quaternary alloys containing various combinations of copper with zinc, tin, and lead is interesting. Quaternary alloys, equivalent to modern "gun metal," seem to have come into use in the 3rd century A.D. and remained popular thereafter, probably because of the working advantages imparted to the copper by addition of all three ingredients. The tin adds strength and hardness to the finished product, the zinc acts as a deoxidant in casting, and the lead increases fluidity of the melt in casting. Whether this practice is owing to the remelting of heterogeneous scrap metals containing these alloying ingredients or whether it is the result of deliberate alloying is unclear. At any rate, it seems that the metalworkers of these periods were able to vary their alloys to suit the kinds of artifacts they were interested in making. Pure copper, for example, is softer and therefore easier to work by hammering than alloyed metal, whereas the casting properties of copper as well as its durability and strength are enhanced by the addition of other elements, such as tin, lead, or zinc (Waldbaum 1983, Chap. V).

With the invasion and destruction of the early 7th century, both the Byzantine shops and the House of Bronzes (and of course the rest of the early Byzantine city of Sardis and the flourishing industries it supported) fell. From that time on the city went into a long decline lasting to the present day. And the material finds of later eras never suggest a return to the earlier prosperity for which we have abundant evidence.

Though the style of material culture differed drastically throughout the millennia, the approach of modern scholars in their attempts to derive the fullest information possible from all forms of evidence is essentially the same. By combining our knowledge of ancient literary and historical sources, inscriptions, archaeological investigations in the field, and geological, chemical, metallurgical, and other kinds of scientific analyses with a thorough study of the objects recovered, from the most elegant to the most mundane, we can reconstruct much of importance in the life of the great city of ancient Sardis.

REFERENCES

Foss, Clive
1976   *Byzantine and Turkish Sardis*. Sardis Monograph 4. Cambridge, Mass.

Greenewalt, C. H., Jr.
1978   The Sardis Campaign of 1976, *BASOR* 229: 57–73.

Herodotus
     The Histories. Translated by A. D. Godley. Loeb Classical Library, 1966.

Waldbaum, Jane C.
1983   *Metalwork from Sardis: The Finds Through 1974*. Sardis Monograph 8. Cambridge, Mass.
1983a   An Unfinished Bronze Ibex from Sardis, *Antike Kunst* 26: 67–72.

ROMAN ARCHITECTURE AT SARDIS

Fikret K. Yegül

The inscription carved on the west side of the Arch of Hadrian in Athens, facing the rocky slopes of the Acropolis, proclaims, "This is Athens, the ancient city of Theseus," and on the east side, "This is the city of Hadrian, not of Theseus." This was, no doubt, a dramatic expression of the emperor's philhellenic feelings as well as an exaggerated announcement of his contributions toward the rebuilding of the city. An arch or a comparable monument, inscribed to express similar sentiments by Roman benefactors, would have been quite appropriate for Sardis or for most of the major cities of western Asia Minor, although a sharp demarcation between the pre-Roman and Roman city might not have been noticeable as it was not even for Athens. Ephesus, Smyrna, Miletus, and Pergamon, all important Hellenistic centers, achieved their greatest prosperity and completed their urban development under Roman rule. And in each, an astounding number of epigraphical records and monuments express civic pride and commemorate individual efforts of rebuilding though rarely with such lofty mythological allusions as the Arch of Hadrian.

In A.D. 17, an earthquake ruined 12 cities of Asia Minor. Sardis was hit hardest; its complete devastation brought the city to imperial attention for special relief measures. According to Tacitus, who gave a vivid account of the disasters, Tiberius granted 10 million sesterces to Sardis and remitted taxes for five years (*Annals* 2,47). A senatorial commissioner, Marcus Ateius, was sent to review the situation and initiate a recovery program.

Insofar as its urban implications are concerned, the earthquake at Sardis can be compared to the Great Fire of Rome in A.D. 64, an event which gave Nero his chance for an ambitious reorganization and rebuilding of the capital. Sardis, like Rome, was almost entirely leveled, the force of the earthquake had even changed landscape forms.   Quite apart from the thankless job of demolition and clearing of unsafe buildings and the creation of city dumps, the salient features of the urban recovery program started by Marcus Ateius and his technicians were the laying out of a major east-west colonnaded avenue (Marble Road), which was crossed at right angles by a secondary, north-south street (East Road).

At the juncture of these thoroughfares, which formed the hub of the new downtown, a colossal bath-gymnasium complex was planned (Figs 7, 32, 40, and 48). By the mid-1st century A.D., the construction of its elaborate substructure was well under way. A statue base dedicated under Claudius (A.D. 47–54) posthumously honored Tiberius as the "founder of the city." It must have been exhibited inside the colonnade of the Marble Road, where it was found (Yegül 1986; Foss 1986). The colonnaded Marble Road of Sardis is one of the earliest examples of the type; interestingly, the better known colonnaded street in Antioch on the Orontes was probably also a Tiberian project (Ward-Perkins 1981). Immediately to the east of the bath-gymnasium complex and the East Road, a public plaza with several civic structures, now hidden by unexcavated but conspicuous hillocks, might have been a part of the Master Plan of Ateius.

It is on one of these major roads, or at their crossing, that a spectacular fountain in the form of intertwined bronze snakes with gilt heads was exhibited. Sometime no earlier than the 4th century A.D., this unusual monument, which must have been one of the many fountains of Roman Sardis, was relocated inside the frigidarium of the bath-gymnasium by Basiliscus, a governor of Lydia. Only the inscribed base of the rededicated fountain was found inside the frigidarium. During late antiquity, when the main water supply system of the city might have fallen into disrepair, the public baths would have been the last to be cut off (Yegül 1986; Foss 1986; Hanfmann and Ramage 1978). The water supply and drainage system of the city seems also to have been a part of the original scheme of Ateius; the construction of the aqueduct which brought water to Sardis was completed under Claudius.

The amplitude, the boldness, and the highly formalized character of the project suggest that it was developed by urban planners in Ateius' professional retinue in consultation with the Imperial Works Office in Rome. There is no question, however, that local architects, engineers, and administrators collaborated in the project and were, perhaps, responsible for the design of individual buildings or for their adaptation to their sites. They must have been also responsible for the daily supervision of the operations. We know one of them, Tiberius Claudius Apollophanes, a Greek by birth but a Roman citizen, who was the supervisor of the construction of the aqueduct (Buckler and Robinson 1932). The important role played by Rome in the creation and approval of large-scale urban schemes in the provinces, as well as its willingness to give free rein to competent provincial architects, is evident in the celebrated correspondence between Trajan and Pliny.

As sweeping and grand as the new scheme for Sardis appears to have been, it did not start from a complete *tabula rasa*. When Ateius began his work he found a city, largely destroyed, but with over half a millennium of urban life and experience. All of the necessary elements of a major center, such as main streets, squares, fountains, and public buildings—a physical and integrated setting described recently by William L. MacDonald as an "urban armature"—already existed in more or less recognizable form.

In any city a set of geographical and historical factors gives tangible shape to its plan and controls its future growth. Sardis was founded at a juncture where the foothills of the Tmolos mountain range, articulated by a dramatic and almost impregnable acropolis, and the valley of the famed "gold-bearing" Pactolus stream, met the fertile Hermus plain (Figs. 32 and 41). These unchangeable features determined the skeletal outline of the city's armature from Lydian days onward: two major roads crossed each other at right angles, an east-west road connecting the inland with the coast and a lesser north-south one following the Pactolus bed over mountain passes to the north. Each artery echoed the flow and alignment of a river, the former the large, slow-moving Hermus in the plain, and the latter its torrential tributary winding its way down among the hills and deep valleys of the Tmolos range. We know that the immediate forerunner of the early imperial colonnaded Marble Road was the Hellenistic-Seleucid east-west road, which seems to have had a bent axis: this road, in turn, must have replaced the famous Royal Road from Susa in Iran to Sardis, constructed under Persian rule in the second half of the 6th century B.C., when Sardis was a satrapal capital (Hanfmann 1983).

It is doubtful that Sardis ever had an orthogonal grid plan, even during the Roman era. Rather, like many other Anatolian citadels and valley towns, such as Magnesia ad Sipylum, Philadelphia, Aigai, and Pergamon, it seems to have adopted the organic and picturesque approach to city planning. With the exception of its two axial arteries, the rest of the street pattern must have followed natural contours, those in a north-south direction across the slopes of the acropolis arranged as steps, or as streets winding down following natural ravines and spurs, with the land between developed as a series of successive terraces.

The Master Plan of Ateius appears to have adapted to and emphasized the bent-axis scheme of its Hellenistic precursor (Fig. 7). The colonnaded Marble

Road extended from the Pactolus almost a mile eastward. At the southeast corner of the bath-gymnasium complex the road bends slightly but perceptibly (ca. 10 degrees) north-northeast and is articulated by a late Roman tetrapylon (four-way arch). It is at this junction that the East Road, colonnaded along the eastern facade of the bath complex, joins the Marble Road (Fig. 40).

The new alignment of the latter parallels that of a number of major Roman and late antique buildings occupying the flat northern quarter of the city. Among them are the basilica, Building C; the so-called Byzantine church D; and the CG baths, the last mentioned not included within the circuit of the late Roman city walls (Fig. 7). Conforming to the same northeastern alignment, a short stretch of marble-paved street was found between Building C and Building D west of a local mill: this could be either the eastern continuation of the Marble Road (leading to an east gate?) or a secondary street roughly parallel to it. A street of late Hellenistic origins, dubbed Street of Pipes, leads diagonally from the Pactolus area toward the east-west road. During the Roman and late antique period, this important street, or another one keeping the same diagonal direction, passed through the southwest gate in the city walls and continued obliquely as a seven-meter-wide, marble-paved, colonnaded street through HOB, linking the Pactolus valley directly with downtown (Hanfmann 1975, 1983; Foss 1976).

The long-term validity of the planning decisions made by Ateius and his professional staff is evident in the archaeological record attesting to the successful development of the Marble Road and the bath-gymnasium complex into a popular commercial, social, and cultural center during the 2nd and 3rd centuries. This probably represents the period of the greatest expansion in the city's history, with an estimated population of 60,000–100,000 (Hanfmann 1983). During the 3rd century, a row of some 34 or 35 shops (Byzantine shops) were built against the south wall of the bath complex and opened into the wide colonnade (Figs. 34, 40, and 48). The contents of the shops indicate that many were engaged in fairly specialized forms of trade and industry: ironsmiths, bronze casters, glass makers and sellers, paint dealers, jewelers, and restauranteurs.

Even more important for the cultural and architectural development of the area was the rebuilding of the entire southern wing of the palaestra of the bath-gymnasium complex sometime at the end of the 3rd century A.D. into a monumental synagogue of the basilica type (Fig. 34) The apsidal main hall (the apse with a tribunal originally belonged to a Roman civil basilica) was approached from the East Road through a forecourt, or anteroom, arranged as a peristyle courtyard with a handsome marble crater fountain in the middle. The colossal size (85 × 20 meters), the desirable position, and the rich decoration of the synagogue (mosaic and marble floors, marble inlaid walls of geometric and figurative designs) offer a firm testimony to the peaceful coexistence of Christian and Jewish populations in late antique Sardis. Quoting Kraabel: "The importance of the discovery of the Sardis synagogue is simply that it reveals a Jewish community of far greater wealth, power, and self confidence than the usual views of ancient Judaism would give us any right to expect."

The ruins of two large buildings with massive ashlar piers in the flat land north of the Marble Road (Buildings C and D), and a string of hillocks to the east and northeast of the East Road, suggest that this area was reserved for public buildings and public spaces comparable to the vast flat area containing the state agora near the east end of Ephesus. Sardis, like Ephesus, must have had a second agora or forum (the old Hellenistic agora? a commercial agora?), possibly located on higher ground, on one of the terraced northern spurs of the acropolis. This is at least hinted at in an inscription which mentions an unidentified building "downroad from the agora"— *kathados agoras* (Buckler and Robinson 1932). Although the reused building blocks and ornament inside the piers of Building D date it no earlier than the end of the 3rd or early 4th centuries A.D., the colossal oblong hall known as Building C is definitely a structure of the mid-empire (Fig. 7). In its great double-apsed hall one can recognize the frigidarium of another bath-gymnasium complex of the imperial type, as imposing as the one we have excavated. If my hypothesis is correct, the heated halls of the new bath would have been arranged toward the south, symmetrical about the main north-south axis of the double-apsed hall. Together with the CG baths, this would give three major bathing complexes to Sardis, not unusual considering Ephesus had some four or five.

If the baths were "secular temples" for Roman society, as phrased by MacDonald, the discovery in 1981 of what appears to be a conventional pseudo-dipteral temple of early or mid-1st century A.D. helps to fill an important void in our knowledge of religious architecture in Roman Sardis. We know that by the 3rd century the city boasted three neocorates, or official temples dedicated to the imperial cult. These temples are represented on the coins of Elagabalus, A.D. 218. The principal, and until recently the only known, temple in Sardis was the temple of Artemis, of Hellenistic origin although the cult and the shrine go back to the Lydian era. This great structure, severely damaged in the earthquake, seems to have taken a long time to be properly repaired and rebuilt. An inscription of Trajanic date carved on one of the new bases proclaims it to be "the first column to rise again." The rebuilding was completed under Antoninus Pius and the new temple was dedicated to the emperor and his wife Faustina.

This was the occasion for which the city was honored with the second neocorate. The newly-discovered pseudodipteros, known only by one corner of its exterior colonnade, is located on one of the natural terraces below the steep northern slopes of the acropolis, at the southern edge of the Roman city, and shares the same orientation with the theater and the stadium (Figs. 7 and 41). It has been tentatively identified as an imperial temple, possibly dedicated to Vespasian (Ratte, Howe, and Foss 1986).

What do we know about domestic architecture in Sardis, and did Ateius' efforts in reorganizing the post-earthquake city include new quarters for housing? We can only supply partial and tentative answers to these questions. We know that the large and congested domestic quarter in the Pactolus valley of the Lydian and early Hellenistic periods had already been abandoned as the late Hellenistic and Roman city shifted eastward. Only during the 4th and 5th centuries A.D. was interest in the Pactolus area revived. A number of villas (one with an elaborate bathing suite) as well as a Constantinian basilical church were built along the eastern bank of the river. A single luxurious residence of the domus type, named House of Bronzes, was excavated in sector HOB, south of the bath-gymnasium complex. This wealthy establishment, with marble floors and servants' quarters, appears to have been an exceptional building in an area which was left quite open and unbuilt during the Roman era, or possibly made into a public park recalling the Lydian and Persian tradition of creating urban parks and gardens (Athenaeus 12.515 d-f; Xenophon *Oeconomicus* 4.20f).

The only substantial evidence for a residential quarter in Roman Sardis comes from the terraced houses on the hills south of HOB, modest units with small courtyards resembling the better-preserved and better-investigated slope houses (*Hanghausern*) in Ephesus. They undoubtedly had late Hellenistic forerunners which were damaged in the earthquake. The area must have been partially filled up with debris during the Roman reshaping of the hillside. These terraced houses, taking full advantage of the beautiful view of the plain and mountains and the cooling afternoon breezes from the west, must have offered a very desirable residential choice for the middle- and upper-income families. The continuation of the residential zone must have extended down the slopes toward the Marble Road and the downtown.

In recent excavations clusters of late Roman houses with small peristyle courtyards, oblong vestibules, and apsidal units have been uncovered in the gently rising hill across from the southeast corner of the bath-gymnasium complex and partially built into the large Lydian mudbrick structure (MMS). These houses, built and occupied during the 4th to 6th centuries, display considerable wealth and refinement. They have marble slab or *opus sectile* (cut marble making geometric patterns) floors, water supply and drainage systems, and, some even have wall paintings (Greenewalt, Rautman, and Meriç 1986).

One can offer the following hypothetical picture as a rough description of the urban form of Roman Sardis. The city was divided by the great colonnaded east-west avenue into two zones of unequal size (Fig. 7). The flat ground north of the Marble Road was the public zone with important civic structures and spaces.

The laying out of this quarter was largely the result of the post-earthquake development, and it presented a more orderly appearance than the rest of the city. The rising ground south of the Marble Road occupied roughly twice as much area as the northern zone and was largely residential. Clusters of single- or double-storied houses with peristyle courtyards hugged the slopes extending down from the steep northern foothills of the Acropolis; the terraced house clusters were broken by irregular, steep, and winding streets and stairs. The overall pattern must have looked quite unclassical, closer to the spirit of traditional Anatolian hill towns with scores of individual residences (and an occasional mosque and minaret) spread over, informally and picturesquely, the hills and valleys, rather than, say, ancient Priene with its ample residential terraces and city blocks arranged in uniform and orderly tiers.

Highlighting the residential arena, perched on prominent natural spurs and nestled in hollows, were some of the larger public buildings and religious precincts, such as the theater, the stadium, temples, clubhouses, meeting halls, stoas, colonnaded belvederes, and gardens. The existence of some of these public structures is known to us only through inscriptions or ancient authors such as a 2nd century A.D. inscription which mentions a tribe (*phyle*) of Dionysias that built for itself a stoa and an exedra attached to a garden. Among other buildings known from inscriptions are the Odeon, Gymnasium of the Elders, the Confraternity Building of Attis, the precinct of Zeus and Men, the temple of Augustus, and the city archives (Buckler and Robinson 1932; Hanfmann 1983).

Culminating this scenographic arrangement was the majestic rise of the acropolis, with a few isolated structures hanging dramatically from its upper slopes. One such building is the so-called North Palace, a terraced structure of fine Lydian masonry situated on the northern heights of the acropolis. Another is lower down the hill, a recently discovered terrace of Lydo-Persian ashlar work, concealed under a massive late Roman wall referred to as the Byzantine Fort. The latter structure, positioned on a prominent natural spur to the west of the theater, could indeed be a logical candidate for the substructures of the legendary palace of Croesus. This venerable building, according to Vitruvius, was extant during his lifetime (late 1st century B.C.), but it had been transformed into the meeting hall for the Council of Elders, or the *Gerousia* (2, 8, 9–10). During the late 3rd or early 4th century A.D., all of this area was enclosed within a fortification wall of mortared rubble.

The most monumental public building, and the best preserved from the Roman period, is the bath-gymnasium complex located at the crossing of the Marble Road and the East Road (Figs. 7, 32, and 34). It is defined by a rectangular outline measuring 120 meters north-south and 170 meters east-west, and occupies roughly 5 1/2 acres (2.07 hectares). The planning of the colossal complex was clearly integrated into the Master Plan of the post-earthquake city.

The groundwork, the construction of the artificial terrace, partly fill and partly supported by concrete barrel vaults, and the laying out of the elaborate subterranean water supply and service system of the baths must have been started under Claudius and continued during the second half of the 1st century A.D. The bath block must have been completed by the middle of the 2nd century as a statue of emperor Lucius Verus (A.D. 161–169) was set up inside the south apse of the great hall BSH and dedicated by Claudius Antoninus Lepidus, the gymnasiarch (Yegül 1986; Foss 1986). The building was in use until the destruction of Sardis in A.D. 616. Some of the major walls of the bath block had always been visible above ground; the ruins were identified as baths by Howard Crosby Butler, the director of the Princeton expedition, 1910–1914. The complex was excavated and partially restored by the Harvard-Cornell expedition, 1958–1975.

The plan of the bath-gymnasium complex at Sardis is recognizable as the "large imperial type," consisting of a series of rooms arranged symmetrically around the main east-west axis (Fig. 34). Almost the entire east half of the complex is occupied by a colonnaded square courtyard, the palaestra, entered from the east through a central gate with triple openings. The vaulted halls of the western half, culminating in a single caldarium, were intended for bathing. On the west side of the palaestra, opposite the east gate, is the Marble Court, a rectangular hall open to the sky displaying a sumptuous architecture of alternating aedieular facades in two stories (Fig. 33). This lavishly decorated space, which appears to have been associated with the Imperial Cult, was reconstructed from the ground up between 1964 and 1973 (Bolgill 1986; Yegül 1986, 1976). According to the dedicatory inscription carved on the first story architrave, the court assumed its present decorative scheme under Septimius Severus and Caracalla, in A.D. 211–212. The same inscription informs us that this act of munificence was undertaken by the city and by two prominent Sardian women, C. Antonia Sabina and Flavia Politte (Foss 1986).

The original scheme in the Marble Court had wide apses in the centers of three walls. The main apse on the west side was framed by a pediment broken by an arch, an architectural motif known as a "Syrian pediment," carried by a double-story order of four spirally-fluted columns of yellow-ochre marble, *giallo antico*, imported from Tunisia. Inside this apse, a statue of the emperor or an altar of the Imperial Cult might have been displayed though none were found in situ. Just such a table-altar decorated with imperial eagles on its supports was reused inside the synagogue next door. And a large marble base which originally belonged to the Marble Court but found inside the frigidarium carried the image of the emperor; inscribed on the base is a dedication to Caracalla (Foss 1986). Sometime in the late 4th or early 5th century the apses were cut through and made into passages, which altered the function of the Marble Court from a cult space into a ceremonial vestibule. This must have been a response to the declining interest during late antiquity in the Imperial Cult.

Halls similar to the Marble Court in design and location occur in most of the imperial bath-gymnasium complexes in Asia Minor. Closest parallels to the Sardis example are the harbor bath-gymnasium, the east baths, and the Vedius bath-gymnasium, all three in Ephesus. In the last mentioned, both an altar for the Imperial Cult and a statue base for the image of Antoninus Pius, to whom the complex was dedicated jointly with Artemis, were discovered in situ inside the central apse. These discoveries led the Austrian excavators to dub these halls *Kaisersale*. The architectural iconography of *Kaisersale*, with their columnar and aedicular elements and rich sculptural decoration, might have alluded to royal and palatial symbolism and singled them out as suitable environments for the unfolding of imperial themes and ideas (Yegül 1982, 1983).

The reconstructed Marble Court offers a palpable example of the growing taste in Roman imperial architecture for rich and decorative facades. The design has a fully baroque feeling, created by the variety of decorative motifs and costly, multicolored marbles. There are plain, fluted, reverse-fluted, and spirally fluted shafts of various colored marbles and porphyries. These shafts rise over simple Attic bases, tall square pedestal bases, or, in a few cases, over drums decorated by rich acanthus foliage resembling Corinthian capitals. There are Ionic, Corinthian, and palmette-and-lotus capitals, and adorning the long screen colonnade separating the court from the palaestra, oval Corinthian capitals displaying sculptured heads (Hirschland 1967; Hanfmann and Ramage 1978).

All this fits very well with the tendency for exuberance that one encounters in Roman architecture of the 2nd and 3rd centuries, especially in Asia Minor, where the vogue toward polychromatic, eye-catching, decorative displays of columnar facades on a variety of building types, such as the stage fronts of theaters, public fountains, and city and market gates, was unusually strong. There is no question that a vital stimulus for such baroque tendencies came from the widespread production and international availability of a large variety of marbles during the 2nd and 3rd centuries A.D. throughout the eastern Mediterranean basin (Ward-Perkins 1951, 1980).

Another important factor must have been the changing aesthetic position of architectural ornament in general. In Sardis, as elsewhere, 3rd century ornament in general, and Severan ornament in particular, reveals considerable roughness of form, reduction of individual motifs and a much coarser but vigorous quality of workmanship compared with the tightly organized and better-crafted work of earlier periods. These characteristics should be regarded as the outcome of the desire to reduce extra work and to achieve a rich effect through deeply undercut, large-featured ornamental motifs which were not intended to be viewed at close quarters. Second and 3rd century Roman ornament was not the creation of sculptors and artists in the sense that Greek or even Augustan ornament was, but merely a part of the cruder art of construction, the decorative extension of that vast, fast-moving imperial building program over three continents (Yegül 1986).

A visitor to the bath-gymnasium complex in the 3rd century would enter the building by passing through the main gates on the east, inside the colonnade along the East Road (Fig. 34). Upon admittance, the visitor would step into an enormous courtyard open to the sky in the middle but enclosed by tall Corinthian colonnades on all four sides. Because some kind of athletic exercise or games preceded hot bathing, Sardians could be seen in the large central area jogging, wrestling, jumping, or engaged in popular forms of ball games—the last preferred by many as a less strenuous form of sport.

Before the newly arrived visitor could join in these activities, he would have to undress and put on a short tunic. The entrance lounges and the changing rooms (*apodyteria*) were situated in the area to the south and north of the Marble Court—barrel-vaulted halls BE-C and BE-CC entered through the vestibules BE-S and BE-N or directly from the palaestra colonnade. Secondary changing rooms might have been located conveniently behind the colonnades, since the palaestra might have served as an independent gymnasium, an educational and athletic facility for the city.

Although the gymnasium as a center for pagan culture and education had no place in the Christian world and athletics as physical cultivation of the body was not tolerated, the palaestras were not simply abandoned. Inscriptions of the 5th century scratched on the *opus sectile* pavement of the Marble Court mention the "place" for the city council and the *gerousia*. Despite the ad hoc nature of these graffiti, they are important reminders of the longevity of these cultural and administrative organizations in the late Roman city and suggest the continued use of the palaestra at Sardis for civic functions long after its athletic meaning had come to an end (Claude 1969; Jones 1964; Yegül 1983).

After exercises in the palaestra, the bathers could enter the bath building and move along one of two symmetrically identical paths which lay north and south of the Marble Court, BE-S/BE-N and BE-C/BE-CC. They could then pass through one of the two long, double-apsed halls BSH/BNH into the heated western part of the complex (Fig. 36). Although the discovery of a statue base of Lucius Verus inside the south apse of BSH gives a ceremonial character to this space, it was perhaps a grand concourse and a general mixing area within the sociable context of Roman baths where, as described by Lucian in *The Baths of Hippias*, bathers could ". . . sit or stand in comfort, linger without dangers and stroll about with profit."

After going through a number of intercommunicating halls constituting the heated western row of the baths, the two paths converged in the single caldarium. One could imagine that in this largest, warmest, and most luminous of bathing halls, under the lofty barrel vaults (23.80 meters high at the intrados), marble piers, and great, arched "thermal" windows, Sardians mingled—washing, wading in the heated pools, exercising vigorously, enjoying a professional massage or a simple backrub, and even eating and drinking in small groups. Judged by Seneca's famous 56th Letter, life in these lavishly decorated and brilliantly lit halls must have been noisy and somewhat hectic, but at the same time full of festive, community spirit, which made visiting the public baths a most pleasurable daily habit, an essential part of Roman life. Leaving the caldarium, the bathers moved back eastward into the large oblong hall BE-H, or the frigidarium, the main hall which offered cold bathing facilities with its numerous unheated pools, private and communal—a rejuvenating termination of the bathing ritual. After the cold bath, a final massage complete with perfumed ointments was enjoyed by many.

Having dressed, the Sardians were now ready to leave the baths and hurry off to dinner. Some probably retired quietly through a minor door in unit BE-A, which led directly into the Marble Road. But the majority might have preferred a more ostentatious exit by way of the palaestra. A few of the *nouveaux riches*, like Petronius' comical hero Trimalchio, might even have been bundled up in soft blankets and carried out on a litter accompanied by a mob of servants, slaves, and well-wishers.

The planning of the bath-gymnasium complex in Sardis represents a direct combination of a Roman bath and the palaestra of a Hellenistic gymnasium. It is a well-established type of bulding which appears quite frequently in many of the cities of Asia Minor. The earliest and clearest example of full axial symmetry in the planning of baths in Asia Minor, and the combination of a vaulted bath building with a palaestra, are the baths of Capito in Miletus. They are firmly dated by a building inscription to the reign of Claudius (A.D. 47–54). More developed examples are to be found in Ephesus, Aphrodisias, Hierapolis, Alexandria Troas and Ankara. The closest planning parallel to the Sardis complex is the Vedius bath-gymnasium at Ephesus. Both of these establishments display a scheme where the bathing and palaestral components have been pulled together and arranged symmetrically along a single, powerful building axis. The Sardis complex represents one of the earliest and perhaps the most organic and sophisticated synthesis of the conventional plans of the palaestra and the thermae connected visually and functionally.

The key position occupied by Asia Minor in the creation of a new architectural type referred to as the bath-gymnasium can be explained by the fact that the people who produced it had two distinct and complementary cultural heritages. While the strong axial symmetry, the daring vaulted spaces, and the advanced technology of these institutions clearly derive from the West and were strongly influenced by the type of imperial thermae developed in Rome by the middle or the second half of the 1st century A. D., the immediate sources for the palaestral component of the ensemble are to be found in the planning of the Greek and Hellenistic gymnasium. Almost from its inception in the 5th and 4th centuries B.C., there was a certain kinship between the gymnasium and heated baths. Throughout the Hellenistic period the bathing component continued to be connected and gradually dominated the athletic function of the gymnasium. In Asia Minor, where Greek culture and its institutions remained vital, the Roman bath and the Hellenistic gymnasium merged into a new, composite architectural type: the bath-gymnasium.

Finally, a word or two must be said about Roman construction in Sardis, where, as it is true for Asia Minor in general, building materials and techniques played a very important part in shaping architecture. A large and well-preserved structure such as the bath-gymnasium complex provides an ideal model for the study of the methods and materials of construction on the site and their development over time.

The structural system of the bath-gymnasium complex can be described as one of load-bearing walls in mortared rubble and brick articulated by ashlar piers (Fig. 36). The weight of the massive vaulting is transferred to the foundations either by individual piers or by pier clusters organized more or less as a frame. In the former, the load imposed by the vaults is not transferred to the piers directly, but first to an upper zone of massive wall section of mortared rubble and brick, about 2.50–3.50 meters thick, which acts as an intermediary structural element distributing the stresses uniformly to the arches and interconnected piers below. The system is the same as that used in the major bathing complexes of Ephesus (where the upper zone construction is usually in solid brick) as well as many other Roman cities in the Meander Valley (Fasolo 1962; Yegül 1986).

The piers are constructed of blocks of limestone or local marble and consist of a rubble and mortar core. The proportion of the core to the exterior ashlar work varies with the size and the structural significance of the piers as well as with their construction date. In general, the piers of the western one-third of the complex supporting vaults over some of its largest interior spans, such as the caldarium, are constructed with larger blocks with carefully trimmed joints fitted together by metal clamps using little or no mortar in the joints and solid cores of ashlar. The piers of the central and eastern zones have smaller blocks, which act as a veneer over a core of rubble. The construction of the western zone was started somewhat earlier than the eastern sections, dating, possibly, to the end of the 1st and early 2nd centuries. All of the relieving arches throughout the complex are in solid brick, arranged in double rings with a 0.40 meter upper ring over a 0.60 meter lower one. Sardis reflects the general tendency in Asia Minor during the imperial era for barrel vaults to cover major spaces, although a few of the halls with square proportions— the vestibules BE-S and BE-N and the great central hall BE-C— utilized cross-vaults or domical vaults. In the latter, true pendentives might have made their first appearance in Roman construction. All vaulting is of brick radially laid with a backing of rubble and mortar, especially at the haunches where compression strengths are necessary.

Two types of walls as infill panels between ashlar piers are used. In the western third of the complex, small, squared blocks were laid in regular horizontal courses, a system known as "petit appareil" and quite typical of western Roman construction, northern Italy, and Gaul during the early Empire (Ward-Perkins 1981). A less careful application of this method can be seen in the Vedius bath-gymnasium in Ephesus. The second system, used far more extensively in the eastern two-thirds of the bath block and in all of the preserved upper zones of walls, is mortared rubble intercepted by horizontal bands of brick. The brick bands were introduced with structural intent, and, unlike their counterparts in the West, they penetrate the entire thickness of the wall. In Sardis, this method, faster and cheaper than "petit appareil" replaced it by the early or mid-2nd century. It enjoyed widespread application in Sardis and in other sites of western coastlands, and formed the basis of Byzantine construction in Asia Minor.

It has been maintained that Roman planning in Asia Minor, particularly the composition of the great bath structures, displays a linear and compartmental quality compared with the more fluent handling of space and structure of the western thermae. This was a response to the limitations set by local materials and techniques, because the builders in Asia Minor lacked the *pozzolana* of central Italy— a volcanic dust which forms an extraordinarily strong bond in Roman concrete— and several generations of experience in concrete technology and vaulting (Ward-Perkins 1981). The bath-gymnasium complex at Sardis is somewhat unusual in that it reveals considerable interest in the use of curvilinear elements such as a pair of double-apsed halls joined by a central hall with a domical vault (BSH-BCH-BNH) (Figs. 34 and 36). This arrangement seems to express a desire to break free from the rectilinear spatial straitjacket— and from the traditional aesthetic deriving from the formal expression of Hellenistic cut-stone construction. Whether other major Roman buildings on the site reveal these characteristics is a question that can be answered only by future excavations and investigations.

The urban pattern established in Sardis as a result of the earthquake of A.D. 17 seems to have been maintained, modified, and enriched throughout the

Empire and late antiquity. After a period of neglect, the Pactolus valley once more assumed prominence as a suburban residential corridor accented with a number of rich villas. The marble paved, colonnaded street cutting northeast from the Pactolus area (from the Hypaepan Gate? A "Hypaipa Street" is mentioned in an inscription; Foss 1976) to the busy southeast corner of the bath-gymnasium complex was rebuilt or restored. The bath-gymnasium and the Byzantine shops continued to flourish even though the gymnasium component of the former (and all other gymnasia in the city) must have been curtailed. Inscriptions attest to the existence of an important arms factory at Sardis under Diocletian and a hospital under Justinian (Buckler and Robinson 1932). Perhaps the best testimony to the urban wealth and vigorous building activity in late antique Sardis is the lengthy inscription of the Builders' and Artisans' Union of A.D. 459 setting forth in clear and detailed language the terms of the professional relationship between workers and employers, a rare and useful document for the economic and architectural history of Asia Minor (Foss 1976; Hanfmann 1983).

It is unlikely that Roman Sardis retained any architectural elements from its pre-Classical and Anatolian past, with the exception, perhaps, of certain isolated cultural and architectural relics (such as the Palace of Croesus or the Pyramid Tomb) or certain ornamental details that escape archaeological record (such as the possible continuation of Lydian terracotta ornament in domestic structures). Its larger urban form, its picturesque and irregular setting, however, took shape in accordance with geographical and historical factors.

Sardis' cultural and religious institutions and its administrative structure bore the stamp of classicism which had been thoroughly embraced by the Lydian city by the 3rd century B.C. The post A.D. 17 reorganization and romanization of Sardis—the building or rebuilding of colonnaded streets, arches, fountains, public squares, temples to the Imperial Cult, baths, gymnasia, basilicas, meeting halls, clubhouses, a theater and a stadium—created the tangible and standard elements of a Roman city fundamentally like so many others in the Empire.

What aspects of its urbanism, if any, made Sardis unique among the other leading cities of the Asian *koine*, all of which competed with equal fervor and similar methods to win favor and recognition in the eyes of the emperor in Rome? The answer to this question must be sought not in the buildings themselves, but in the intangible realm, in the idea of Sardis as city in the thought of its citizens. For generations of its inhabitants and for the greater Classical world, "golden Sardis" had never lost its historical and mythological allure as the royal capital of the mighty Lydian empire and as the beloved city of Croesus. It was famed for its riches and luxuries as well as for the sophisticated and notorious manners of its citizens. Time and time again its legendary and romantic past was evoked in literature and poetry resurrecting feelings of pan-Lydianism and rekindling the city's pride: ". . . under the flowering Tmolus, beside the stream of Maeonian Hermus" Sardis was the first witness of Zeus and the first nurse of Dionysus (*Anthologia Graeca* IX, 645; Foss 1976; Hanfmann 1983).

It was this aspect of Sardis, the Sardis which lived in myth, legend, and nostalgia, in the words of the late George M. A. Hanfmann, its foremost modern scholar and excavator, the "imaginary Sardis," that gave the city a unique sense of its position in the contemporary Roman world. As late as the Severan period, Sardis winked back to its royal past by calling itself the "metropolis of Greece, of Asia, of all Lydia" and continued to live not under but *with* the shadow of its monumentality until its final destruction by the armies of the Persian king Chosroes II in A.D. 616.

REFERENCES

Bolgil, M. C.
  1986   The Reconstruction of the Marble Court and Adjacent Areas, *The Bath-Gymnasium at Sardis*. Sardis Report 3.   Cambridge, Mass.
Buckler, W. H and D. M. Robinson
  1832   *Sardis VII, Greek and Latin Inscriptions, Part I*. Leyden.
Fasolo, F.
  1962   L'Architettura Romana di Efeso, *Bolletino del Centro di Studi dell'Architettura* 18: 1–92.
Foss, C.
  1976   *Byzantine and Turkish Sardis*. Sardis Monograph 4. Cambridge, Mass.
  1986   Appendix: Inscriptions Related to the Complex, *The Bath-Gymnasium Complex at Sardis*. Sardis Report 3. Cambridge, Mass.
Greenewalt, C. H., Jr, M. L. Rautman, and R. Meriç
  1986   The Sardis Campaign of 1983, *BASOR Supplement* 24: 1–30.
Hanfmann, G. M. A.
  1975   *From Croesus to Constantine*. Ann Arbor.
  1983   *Sardis from Prehistoric to Roman Times*. Cambridge, Mass.

Hanfmann, G. M. A. and N. H. Ramage
    1978   *Sculpture from Sardis: The Finds through 1975.* Sardis Report 2. Cambridge, Mass.

Hanfmann, G. M. A. and J. C. Waldbaum
    1975   *A Survey of Sardis and the Major Monuments Outside the City Walls.* Sardis Report 1. Cambridge, Mass.

Hirschland, N. L.
    1967   The Head-Capitals from Sardis, *BSR* 35: 12–22.

Kraabel, A. T.
    1983   Impact of the Discovery of the Sardis Synagogue, *Sardis from Prehistoric to Roman Times.* Cambridge, Mass.

MacDonald, W. L.
    1986   *The Architecture of the Roman Empire II: An Urban Appraisal.* New Haven.

Ratte, C., T. N. and C. Foss
    1986   An Early Imperial Pseudodipteral Temple at Sardis, *AJA* 90: 45–68.

Ward-Perkins, J. B.
    1951   Tripolitania and the Marble Trade, *JRS* 41: 89–104.
    1980   The Marble Trade and Its Organization: Evidence from Nicomedia, *MAAR* 36: 325–38.
    1981   *Roman Imperial Architecture.* New York.

Yegül, F. K.
    1976   The Marble Court of Sardis and Historical Reconstruction, *JFA* 32: 169–94.
    1982   A Study in Architectural Iconography: *Kaisersaal* and the Imperial Cult, *ArtB* 64.1: 7–31.
    1983   The Bath-gymnasium Complex, *Sardis from Prehistoric to Roman Times.* Cambridge, Mass.
    1986   *The Bath-Gymnasium Complex at Sardis.* Sardis Report 3. Cambridge, Mass.

THE SYNAGOGUE AT SARDIS: JEWS AND CHRISTIANS

A. Thomas Kraabel

Let us begin with a certain hundred years, those from the middle of the 2nd century of the Common Era to the middle of the 3rd. In the year 150 the Jews of the Holy Land were still trying to recover after the second of two disastrous wars with Rome. Jewish militancy was over. Jews as a nation would conduct no such battles again until the establishment of the state of Israel in our own time. The center of nation and cult, the Temple in Jerusalem was in ruins and under gentile control; it would not be rebuilt. Within a century, however, the Mishnah, the text at the heart of post-biblical Jewish teachings, would receive its final form in the Galilee at the hands of the great Rabbi Judah "the Prince."

Just beyond the boundaries of the Holy Land, in the Roman garrison town of Dura Europos, another Judaism was preparing to express itself in much different fashion, in wonderful folk art; the congregants of the little Dura synagogue would cause its walls to be covered with glorious frescoes of biblical symbolism. Varieties of Judaism also flourished west of Dura and the Holy Land, all around the Mediterranean rim, where Jews lived as one of many minorities in the cities of the Roman world.

Among Christians the various documents which would make up the present New Testament had only just been completed by the year 150, along with other Christian texts of many kinds. However, the decisions which would place certain texts into the Christian Bible were only just beginning to be made; the debates would continue for a century and a half. In Asia Minor and then in Rome, Marcion, a bright disciple of Saint Paul, was arguing that the scripture of the Jews, the "Old Testament," had no place in Christianity; the God it described,

Yahweh, was in fact sub-Christian, and His followers were to be repudiated by proper members of the Church. It was Marcion himself who was finally repudiated, after some debate. Meanwhile, many Christians in Asia Minor were setting the date of Easter with the help of the old Jewish calendar, for they believed that to be proper according to the earliest Christian tradition. This "Jewish" practice was frequently the cause for dispute with Christians to the west, for Christianity, which had begun as a Jewish sect in the Holy Land, was now almost exclusively gentile, its centers of power and growth farther west in the gentile world.

Christians were increasingly in conflict with the Roman State and with local authorities. Polycarp, Bishop of Smyrna, not far to the west of Sardis on the coast of Asia Minor, died a martyr in his city in the middle of the 2nd century. But for the Roman Empire in general, the year 150 was a time of prosperity, growth, and peace. The emperor was the conscientious Antoninus, nicknamed Pius. His successor would be his adopted son, the introspective stoic philosopher Marcus Aurelius.

The historian Edward Gibbon called this period the most prosperous age the world had ever known. But there was a whiff of smoke in the air, and flames were apparent at the edges of things. Marcus Aurelius wrote much of his immortal *Meditations* in his field tent, on campaign against the enemies of the Empire and often on its farthest borders. His successor, Commodus (ruled 180–192), saw the beginning of decline, and things grew significantly worse in the early 3rd century. In the half-century before Diocletian, who ruled from 284 to 305, every emperor died by violence, and the average length of reign was two or three years. (It was Diocletian who would conduct the last systematic persecution of Christians).

There was more order, but not much less violence, when Constantine took over less than a decade after Diocletian and began to make Christianity the new state religion.

Somewhere in the hundred years between 150 and 250 the Jewish community at Sardis created its magnificent synagogue. By the year 200, Jews had lived in Sardis for half a millennium or more. They enjoyed a striking amount of acceptance, respect, and indeed power within the city and within the Roman province. Their central artifact is of course the synagogue itself, crammed with gorgeous decoration and many more Jewish inscriptions than are known from all the rest of Asia Minor put together. On the basis of this new evidence and what was previously known about the context of Sardis, it is possible to offer a hypothetical, but very detailed, reconstruction of the Jewish community, its piety, its economics, and its life among gentile neighbors. The purpose of this essay is to summarize that fascinating story.

As any present-day visitor to Sardis can attest, the reconstruction of the synagogue gives a vivid picture of what it must have been originally. No one riding the intercity buses from Ankara to Izmir today can fail to be impressed by the massive structure that looms up on the right a few kilometers west of Salıhlı (Fig. 40). As Yegül indicated in his chapter, the basilica which would become the synagogue was not a freestanding building but, rather, the southeast unit of the huge bath-gymnasium complex shown in Fig. 34. Stage 1 (Fig. 38) shows what had been the original intent: a row of three large rooms opening north into the gymnasium *palaestra*. But at some point during the construction the plans were changed. Stage 2 (Fig. 38) represents the result: a civil basilica with a small forecourt in the east end and, in the west end, an apse provided with a platform or stage looking out over a long, narrow hall. Niches in the wall of the apse contain statues of deities or emperors.

This is the first phase actually put to use by the people of Sardis, beginning somewhere in the 2nd century. That is, from the beginning, Sardis knew this space as a basilica, accessible to all but only from the street to the east, from outside the bath-gymnasium. From the beginning it differed from the parallel hall to the north, the three rooms of which always opened into the palaestra itself.

In the second phase of use, Stage 3 (Fig. 38), a three-tiered bank of semicircular benches was added to the apse, and the crosswall separating the main hall from the forecourt was removed, creating a single hall over 80 meters long from east to west. It was at some point during this phase that the space came under the control of the Jewish community. After it became their synagogue, however, it was still not out-of-bounds to Sardis gentiles. The basilica had been city property for too long to imagine that once in Jewish hands it would be closed to the rest of the city forever. The "fountain of the synagogue" was surely public, and it seems unlikely that Jews whose community had been a part of the city for half a millennium would totally exclude their gentile neighbors from what would now be the center of Jewish life in Sardis.

The third phase of use is the one which has been reconstructed: Stage 4 (Fig. 38), dating from the 4th century. Congregants and visitors entered from the east, from the same colonnaded street which served the palaestra; their entrances were less than 50 meters apart. Three doorways led into the synagogue forecourt, an attractive space roofed on four sides but open to the sky over the fountain in the center. The west wall of the forecourt was pierced by another three doorways leading into the main hall (Fig. 41).

Just inside the main hall were two marble Torah Shrines, one on each side of the central entrance (Fig. 42). The south shrine was evidently the more important; the construction was of better quality, and the few fragments of Hebrew inscription from the building were found here. When the Scripture was to be read aloud from the apse at the west end of the building, the proper scroll must have been brought, perhaps in a formal procession, from one of these shrines. Afterward it would be returned in the same fashion.

Many synagogues today have only one shrine, or Ark, or *Aron ha-Kodesh*, but the Sardis Jews erected two, probably for reasons of symmetry. The shrines and the cross-wall between the forecourt and the main hall are new in this stage of the building. They indicate architecturally the increasing importance of the Scripture, and permit the scrolls to be stored on the wall closest to Jerusalem, a synagogue feature as common in the Diaspora as in the Holy Land. The Sardis Jews had a significant name for such a structure; in one of the inscriptions it is called a *nomophylakion*, "that which protects the Law."

West of the shrines, precisely in the center of the main hall, is the synagogue's most important inscription, introducing "Samoe, priest and *sophodidaskalos*." Sacrificial ritual had ended among Jews centuries before Samoe, when the Temple in Jerusalem was destroyed by Roman armies. A priest is never essential to the function of a synagogue, but Samoe was a descendant of the biblical high priest Aaron and bore the title proudly. *Sophodidaskalos* means "wise teacher" or "teacher of wisdom," and it is likely that Samoe was the closest thing Sardis had to a rabbi.

The west end of the synagogue was the architectural focus of the building. For the services, important members of the community and honored guests were seated on the benches of the apse. They looked out across the semicircular apse mosaic, over the apse railing and the massive lectern and out to the rest of the congregation. The lectern was actually a colossal stone table, dubbed the "Eagle Table" after the massive Roman eagle depicted on the supports at each end—architectural fragments from earlier Roman times in reuse (Fig. 44). The table was flanked by pairs of marble lions, also in reuse, but still earlier, from the Lydian period. A large stone menorah discovered in the excavations may have stood on a small, carefully carved monument discovered nearby. The menorah bears its donor's name: Sokrates.

Eagles, lions, and menorah were all rich in symbolism for the assembled community. At the proper time in the service, the scroll of the Scriptures was unrolled on the Eagle Table. A member of the community stood on a small pedestal at the table, his back to the apse, and read aloud the text designated for the day.

It would be a mistake to see this building as primarily cultic in purpose, like the Jerusalem Temple or an early Christian church. In the Greco-Roman world outside the Holy Land, Jews like those responsible for the Sardis synagogue are best understood not as a religious movement but as an ethnic minority, albeit one with some unusual religious practices. It is important to realize that this building was the only one controlled by the Sardis Jewish community in this period, and that most if not all of the activities of the community would have taken place within it.

A similar situation obtained even before this building existed: according to a Roman decree from the 1st century B.C., the Sardis Jews had been given their own "place" or "location" where decisions were made on community matters, religious and non-religious. This earlier meeting place could have been an entire building, an assembly hall, the forerunner of the mammoth synagogue described above, or it may have been nothing more than a designated space in some public building.

Several features of the present Sardis synagogue recall the famous diplostoon or double-colonnaded synagogue at Alexandria destroyed by Trajan. The Talmud indicates that people seated themselves in the Diplostoon by trades—all the goldsmiths together, all the weavers together, all the carpet makers together—so that a new person in the community associated himself with others in his profession in order to gain employment. Indeed the Sardis synagogue may have functioned as a kind of hiring hall. It was also a school. It may have been used on occasion as a dining hall. And because a main highway from the Aegean to the Holy Land and the east was just outside, Jewish travelers may have spent the night in the building as guests of the Jewish community.

The occupations of Jews in this part of the ancient world are not much different from those of gentiles. There is no indication at Sardis that particular crafts were associated with Jews. Goldsmiths must have been in demand; three of the synagogue donors were Jews of that occupation. Others were merchants; some sold glass, some paints, and some dyes. One may have been a sculptor, others held government positions.

It is their status in the city and the government which Sardis Jews stress in the synagogue inscriptions. Many donors proudly identify themselves as a "citizen of Sardis," and no less than nine use the privileged title "city council member." Perhaps because of their wealth, these individuals must have possessed considerable social status. In addition, three donors were part of the Roman provincial administration: one was a "count," another a procurator, and the third an assistant in the state archives.

The Sardis Jewish community must have been a strong and influential one to gain control of such a large and impressive building. One reason for its strength in the city was the Jewish community's long history, which may have begun as early as the 6th century B.C. The book of Obadiah in the Hebrew Bible mentions (verse 20) exiles from Jerusalem who lived in Sepharad after the Babylonian destruction of Jerusalem in 587. Sepharad is the Semitic name for Sardis.

Another group of Jews settled in the area three centuries later. In an effort to pacify Lydia and Phrygia to the east by increasing the number of his own supporters there, the Seleucid King Antiochus III brought in 2,000 loyal Jewish families from his forces in Babylonia and Mesopotamia, provided them with houses, and gave them a decade's relief from taxation. Because Sardis was the headquarters of the Seleucid governor responsible for these immigrants, it is likely that some of them came to settle in the city.

In all probability it was descendants of this group who established the meeting "place" or "location" whose existence was later guaranteed by the Roman decree mentioned above. This would have been the first Sardis "synagogue." There must have been another as well, whatever building or meeting place was utilized by the community after most of Sardis had been heavily damaged by the earthquake of 17 C.E. This would have been the second Sardis "Synagogue." The third would be the presently reconstructed 3rd–4th century building. Sardis thus had a series of at least three synagogues or Jewish community assembly sites, even more if the history is more complex than what has been sketched here.

The present building and its inscriptions are the central artifact of Sardis Judaism. When these data are taken together with the literary evidence, Jewish, Christian, and pagan, the story of this community's life is expanded considerably.

These Jews were apparently on good terms with their gentile neighbors in Sardis. For one thing, this community— like others in the Diaspora— had the support of the Roman government. Jews were a powerful enough minority within the Empire that the Romans usually preferred to placate them rather than risk their destabilizing the status quo. On the Empire's eastern border the Jewish homeland provided an essential buffer to such enemies of Rome as the Parthians farther to the east. It was when this bulwark seemed at risk, and the eastern frontier less secure, that the situation between Roman troops and Palestinian Jews moved from uneasy truce to pitched battle in the two "Jewish wars" of the 1st and 2nd centuries C.E. It is significant that the Jews of the western Diaspora did not take part in either case, nor did peaceful Jewish communities like the one at Sardis suffer at Roman hands thereafter. (Alexandria in Egypt was always a more volatile city; in that explosive atmosphere, Jews and gentiles suffered more from civil strife).

In addition to Roman support, the Sardis Jews had their own sources of power, both economic and political. This is clear from the evidence of the inscriptions, already mentioned, and from the grandeur of the synagogue itself. Had this not been a strong community in the 2nd and 3rd centuries, the building would likely not have become theirs.

Some of that stature was due to the community's long history in Sardis. They were not aliens; by this time they belonged in the Lydian city. Their long history there was one of the factors recognized by the transfer of the building to their possession. Relative newcomers are unlikely to have been given such an opportunity. To an extent unparalleled elsewhere among the Jews of the Roman Empire, this Jewish community was fully a part of the gentile city which was its home.

If the Jews fit into the larger life of Sardis so well, does that mean they had cut their ties with the homeland? Did Sardis Jews abandon the Holy Land in which their religion centered in order to take up membership in Anatolian gentile society? That might seem likely, particularly when it is recalled that this community may not have begun out of Palestine, but rather from Babylonia and Mesopotamia, the result of the action of Antiochus III already described. But the break with the Holy Land never occurred; the Jews of this community never lost their roots. (I have argued elsewhere that this may have been because the community grew out of another Exile, that is, from Jews who had learned the importance of their heritage in exile when they were taken as hostages to Babylon after the capture of Jerusalem and the destruction of the first Temple there in the late sixth century B.C. I suspect too that by the 3rd and 4th centuries C.E., a millennium later, the real tie was not so much to the Palestine of their own times as it was to biblical Israel raised to mythic status [Kraabel 1987, see also Nickelsburg 1981, Collins 1983].)

Another piece of evidence for the importance of this link is financial. Sardis Jews faithfully donated the annual half-shekel offering for the support of a Temple in Jerusalem, a privilege guaranteed them by the Roman government according to a decree preserved from the 1st century B.C. Other communities did as well, according to evidence provided unwittingly by the great Roman lawyer and politician Cicero. One of the best known incidents in the life of Anatolian Jews occurred in the first century B.C.: the attempt by the Roman governor Lucius Valerius Flaccus to divert to his own use the gold these Jews were sending to Jerusalem to support the Temple. When prosecuted, Flaccus engaged Rome's most famous lawyer to defend him; Cicero's successful speech in Flaccus' defense, the *Pro Flacco*, can still be read. Jewish funds deposited in four cities are mentioned there, two in the interior in Phrygia east of Sardis, and two in Mysia on the northwest coast (Leon 1960). The speech reveals two things relevant to our story. These Jews took their traditional obligations seriously; although far from ancient Palestine, they had not cut their ties to Jerusalem. And collectively they had substantial disposable income; over 200 pounds of gold are involved in the suit. It was not only the Romans in Sardis who controlled funds in quite respectable amounts.

Pilgrimage was another important link to the homeland from the Diaspora, particularly at the annual observances of the three major pilgrim festivals, *Pesah* (Passover), *Shavuout* (Pentecost), and *Sukkot* (Tabernacles). Sardis was located on the main land route for pilgrims coming from the west, and members of the Sardis Jewish community must have been among these pilgrims on occasion. The only Sardian who claimed to have traveled to the Holy Land, however, is the 2nd century Christian Bishop Melito (Kraabel 1971).

We know little about traffic from the other direction. Even though Asia Minor and Sardis were on the edge of the rabbinic world, little attention is paid to this area in rabbinic literature. (Even the meaning of the term "Asia" in the literary evidence is unclear; sometimes it designates what we have been calling Asia Minor, sometimes a single city, sometimes a non-Anatolian location). Rabbinic texts tell of rabbis sent into the Diaspora to collect funds and to keep the official ritual calendar synchronized with that of the Holy Land. The famous 2nd century rabbi Meir once went to "Asia" for the second purpose. The story goes that when he found the community there without a copy of the Book of Esther (for the Purim festival) he wrote one out from memory. Meir is also reported to have died in "Asia." Did these two events take place in the same area or the same city? If an Anatolian community lacked Esther, was it because the community was so far out of touch with the majority of Jews as even to lack a complete text of the Scriptures? Or was it because the people of "Asia" refused to accept the festival of Purim because of its political and anti-gentile emphases, that is, not because they were marginal Jews but because their kind of Judaism was self-consciously independent of the nationalism of the Palestinian homeland?

The most convincing evidence for the allegiance of the Sardis Jews to their traditions and their origins remains the synagogue itself, a building where the community assembled at the appointed times, where the Torah was central, where Samoe (and others) taught, and where in the architecture itself, in the Torah shrines, the connection with Jerusalem was maintained.

And yet Sardis Jews remained open to, indeed at home in, a world where gentiles were the vast majority. This rhythm of allegiance to one's origins and openness to one's neighbors may seem contradictory, and surely was not always easy to maintain. But it was the key to the continued existence of the Jewish community. To relinquish either, and thus to relax the tension, would have meant the disappearance of the Jews of Sardis.

A final reason for the tie to the Holy Land is one not often recognized. In the Mediterranean world *antiquity* was important. In Greco-Roman culture it helped to have a long history. This is what Homer represented for the Greeks. The parallel story for Rome was given classic form by Virgil in the Aeneid. Egypt's great age was respected, and so was Israel's. When the Jews of Sardis claimed Israel's history as their own, they were signaling that they too had their proper place in the vast Greco-Roman civilization.

There were also Christians at Sardis, from the earliest times of the history of the Church. Christian missionaries could reach the city easily via the Roman road system. The first ones had arrived by the middle of the 1st century, that is, they were contemporaries of the Apostle Paul. By the last decade of the 1st century, when the community received the letter to it preserved in the New Testament (Revelation 3:16), it had been in existence long enough to have a good reputation, which it no longer deserved; there had been a decline from earlier accomplishments. Sardis was thus a very early Christian center of some importance. One of its bishops, Melito, was highly influential in the late 2nd century and thereafter, not always in happy ways. The strength of Sardis Christianity increased greatly after Constantine. Sometime late in his reign, or perhaps under his sons, the decision was made to build an entire "Christian quarter" just outside the city gate.

While the Jews might have wanted to ignore this new movement and maintain their life in Sardis as it had continued for centuries, Christians could not really afford to leave Jews undisturbed. Once Christianity moved out of its Jewish context in the Holy Land west to areas where gentiles were greatly in the majority, its ties with Judaism became a problem and soon an embarrassment for Christians. The Christian claim that Jesus was the Christ, the Messiah whom the Hebrew scriptures had promised, was rejected by nearly all Jews. In the Holy Land, where the first followers of Jesus constituted a sect among other Jewish sects, this was in one sense an internal disagreement, a "family argument"—and there had been plenty of those in the Jewish homeland! But in the gentile world the problem of credibility arose very quickly. Christians, whether of Jewish or of gentile descent, made the same assertions: Jesus was the Jews' Messiah, and he matches the promises—or fits the pattern—of the Hebrew Scriptures. Diaspora Jews rejected both claims and in the process forthrightly distinguished themselves from the followers of Jesus. One result was that the protection and patronage the Roman government had provided to Jews would not be available to Christians even if they were of Jewish descent. Further, the assertion of antiquity, of having a long and illustrious past, was blocked for Christians if they could not claim somehow to be "Jewish." The only "past" the Christians had was that of the Old Testament Israelites. If that was not available to them, their standing in the ancient world became even more precarious (*Anti-Judaism* 1986).

Eventually Christianity would sort these things out, but in the early centuries they were acute concerns. And of course they were *Christian* problems, coming from the Christian side, from Christians' understanding of who they were and whence they had come. There were no parallel concerns from the side of the Diaspora Jews.

They became problems very early, too, as soon as the Christian mission was catapulted into the Diaspora. And Asia Minor was one of the very first places these missionaries reached after they left the Holy Land.

One of Bishop Melito's sermons from the later 2nd century still survives, and it is such a violent attack on Jews and on "Israel" that it earned him the title "the first poet of deicide," that monstrous charge that because of the Crucifixion *all* Jews were guilty of "murdering God" (Werner 1966). The impression Melito creates is one of great hostility between Christianity and Judaism at Sardis. That image is suspect, as are suggestions of similar conflict elsewhere. I say this because Christianity was not often an issue for Diaspora Jews in this period. In the beginning Christians were not very numerous in the world of Diaspora Judaism. Later most Christians there were gentiles, as Christianity quickly became a gentile religion. For Christian leaders Judaism did matter, for the reasons given earlier. Most responded with hostility. While Melito's attack is one of the earliest and most bitter, it is not at all isolated. (Kraabel 1971, 1985).

The Christian laity, however, may have been of a different mind, at least at Sardis. Theological issues may have been less important for them. And Jews had been a part of the city's life centuries longer than Christianity had. Jews and Christians (and pagans) had shops side-by-side just outside the bath-gymnasium complex and the synagogue. The central location of the synagogue makes it unlikely that there was anything like a "Jewish quarter" or ghetto there.

And there is one last piece of evidence that Jews and Christians may have lived in relative harmony in this city. The synagogue itself, though it would have made a wonderful church, was never taken over for that purpose. To the end of Sardis' history, when the city was destroyed by Persian forces in 616, three centuries after Constantine, the building remained in Jewish hands.

The Sardis Jews are not the typical example of life in the Greco-Roman Diaspora; there is no such typical community known to me. But with their centuries-long history there, their economic and political substance, their combination of an integration into gentile life with a concern for their "roots," their own history and traditions, they do not fit the traditional stereotype of the frightened and powerless minority lost in a sea of non-Jews and yearning to return to their Homeland. The silent evidence from Sardis deserves to be heard in more places in our own world. I hope you are grasped by their story, and never quite forget them.

REFERENCES

Anti-Judaism
    1986   *Anti-Judaism in Early Christianity.* Studies in Christianity and
                Judaism 2–3. 1. *Paul and the gospels,* edited by P. Richardson and
                D. Granskou. 2. *Separation and Polemic,* edited by S. G. Wilson.
                Waterloo, Ontario.
Collins, J. J.
    1983   *Between Athens and Jerusalem.* New York.
Foss, C.
    1976   *Byzantine and Turkish Sardis.* Cambridge, Mass.
Green, W. S. (ed.)
    1985   *Approaches to Ancient Judaism. V. Studies in Judaism and Its
                Greco-Roman Context.* Atlanta.
Hanfmann, G. M. A.
    1983   *Sardis from Prehistoric to Roman Times.* Cambridge, Mass.
Kraabel, A. T.
    1971   Melito the Bishop and the Synagogue at Sardis: Text and Context.
                Studies Presented to George M. A. Hanfmann. Edited by D. G.
                Mitten, J. G. Pedley and J. A. Scott. Cambridge, Mass.
    1979   The Diaspora Synagogue. *Aufstieg und Niedergang der
                roemischen Welt: Geschichte und Kultur Roms im Spiegel der
                neueren Forschung,* II.19.1.
    1982   The Roman Diaspora: Six Questionable Assumptions. *Journal of
                Jewish Studies* 33: 445–64.
    1983   Impact of the Discovery of the Sardis Synagogue. In Hanfmann
                1983.
    1985   *Synagoga Caeca.* Systematic Distortion in Gentile
                Interpretations of Evidence for Judaism in the Early Christian
                Period. *To See Ourselves As Others See Us: Christians, Jews,
                "Others" in Late antiquity.* Edited by Jacob Neusner and Ernest S.
                Frerichs. Chico, Ca.
    1987   Unity and diversity Among Diaspora Synagogues. In the
                Synagogue in Late Antiquity, edited by L. I. Levine. New York.
                Forthcoming.
Leon, H. J.
    1960   *The Jews of Ancient Rome.* Philadelphia.
Millar, F.
    1967   *The Roman Empire and Its Neighbors.* New York.
Neusner, J.
    1985   The Experience of the City in Late Antique Judaism. In Green
                1985.
Nickelsburg, G.
    1981   *Jewish Literature Between the Bible and the Mishnah.*
                Philadelphia.
Werner, E.
    1966   Melito of Sardis, the First Poet of Deicide. *Hebrew Union College
                Annual* 37: 191–210.

Yegül, F. K.
    1986   *The Bath-Gymnaisum Complex at Sardis.* Sardis Report 3.
                Cambridge, Mass.

SARDIS IN THE BYZANTINE AND TURKISH ERAS

Jane Ayer Scott

Augustus, the first of the Roman emperors, proudly claimed to have found Rome a city of brick and left it a city of marble. The grandeur of imperial planning under the Julio-Claudian emperors who succeeded him extended to the great cities of Asia Minor. The streets of Roman imperial Sardis gleamed with marble colonnades, and the grand interiors were aglow with designs of cut colored stones on walls and floors.

One wonders, however, how deeply Roman styles and institutions penetrated the indigenous population. The 5th century A.D. saw a great deal of building, but brick was the fabric of the late Roman and early Byzantine city. Roman culture may have been as thin a veneer as the marble slabs that covered the brick and as fragile as the plaster and tile that came to replace interior decoration of cut stone. When the imperial presence of Rome and Byzantium faded completely, a vernacular architecture emerged in the village houses which is remarkably similar to that of the ancient Lydians as described by Vitruvius (2.8.9-10; Ramage 1975). Roman pottery types and styles are replaced by glazed wares having patterns that hark back to those in fashion before the conquest of Alexander the Great merged all Asia Minor with the world of Greek and then Roman styles and institutions.

The transition of the great Roman city of Sardis to a cluster of small villages set along the Ottoman road that followed the route of the Roman east-west highway and to the south of it along the banks of the Pactolus stream was not an even continuum of decline. After the Severan period there was a time of crisis from A.D. 235 to 284 when Diocletian took the throne and made Sardis the capital of his new province of Lydia. Diocletian established an imperial weapons and shield factory, or *fabrica*, at Sardis, one of only three in Asia Minor. Raw material was provided by the state and skilled personnel would have been needed in quantity for the weapons manufacture (Waldbaum 1982). The economic impact of this installation may well have been the basis of the prosperity and increase in the population that is evident in a burst of building in the 5th century. The early Byzantine city is estimated to have occupied three square miles.

Some historians do not begin the Byzantine period until the reign of Heraklius (610–641), and numismatists would move up its start to the monetary reforms of Anastasius in the very end of the 5th century, A.D. 491. Others take the establishment of Constantinople, the new capital of Constantine the Great in the East, in 320 as the start of the Byzantine epoch. The seeds of Byzantine life and society can be seen at Sardis in the vigorous building and expansion that occurred in the 5th century and even in the 4th, when Christianity took hold after Constantine made Sardis a metropolis of his church in 312. One of the earliest known Christian basilicas (EA on the site plan, Figs. 7 and 45) was built on the east bank of the Pactolus stream, outside the late antique city wall, and a Christian quarter grew up around it over an area that had been left unoccupied, except by graves, since the Hellenistic period. Here a phase of Constantinian activity may be studied that is not known elsewhere in Asia Minor (Hanfmann 1983).

The Jews of Sardis adapted a ready-made Roman civil basilica with forecourt, main hall, and apse for their synagogue (Kraabel, herein). Soon after "the peace of the church," the acceptance of Christianity by the emperor, the Christians built afresh in an area long unoccupied. The architectural form of their early church was essentially the same: in its original phase it was composed of a basilica with single apse, nave with two aisles lined with colonnades, and a narthex or entrance porch. The patterns of the mosaic floor, vine scrolls, squares, and lozenges echo those of the synagogue and gymnasium. Hans Buchwald (forthcoming) believes that this original part of the church was built in the two decades following 340. If his dating is correct, it is one of the very few known churches outside of Rome, Syria, and the Holy Land assigned to the 4th century and one of the earliest dated churches in Asia Minor. The construction of this basilica inaugurated a sequence of Christian architecture that lasted just short of a millennium of which excavation has revealed only selected vignettes.

Two martyrs from Sardis, victims of the persecutions of the 3rd century, are known to have been canonized, Therapon, a priest, and Apollonius, about whom nothing more is known (Foss 1976). It is possible that the Christians built their church in a cemetery because martyrs such as these were buried there.

If the area opposite the bath-gymnasium and the synagogue did indeed remain open until the early 5th century, as suggested below, the builders had the option to locate the church prominently near the east-west road within the city center. No saint is identified with any of the churches, and the early basilica remains known only by the designation EA, provided by the unimaginative excavators.

From the beginning of the 5th century one can trace additions to the building, an atrium which was entered through a door in the north wall, possibly the major entrance to the church, and to the north a chapel with rooms on its west side. The first Christian church was built under Constantine, the emperor who first embraced Christianity, or his sons. A pause in Christian expansion toward the end of the century probably reflects the return to paganism of the emperor Julian, called the "Apostate" (reigned 360–363) and then in the 5th century the process of Christianization is rapid and unhampered. In addition to building, the use of ritual and utilitarian objects with Christian symbols flourished (Fig. 51).

To the north of the church, across the street, a suite of rooms, probably a villa, was built early in the 5th century, at the same time additions were being made to the church. The mosaic floors are the most interesting discovered at Sardis. They show a centered eagle in a circular frame, surrounded by animals running in the woods and dolphins, each creature within an ornate frame of interlace patterns (Fig. 46).

Remains of foundations, pottery, and mosaic paving visible in the bank of the Pactolus show that this quarter extended south along the stream to the temple of Artemis and beyond. The hypocaust floor of a bath has been identified in one of the villas. Houses and vaulted tombs surrounded the temple. The temple itself was not converted to a church, as was frequently the case, for instance at Aphrodisias where Aphrodite's temple was transformed to the Church of St. Michael (Erim 1986). A small church (Fig. 50), possibly a mortuary chapel, was built into the southeast corner of the colonnade in the 5th century and enlarged in the 6th (Hanfmann 1983). The temple itself was partly filled in, and graves encroached on the precinct by the mid-4th century. Crosses were etched on the visible walls of the temple to sanctify it.

Brick vaulted tombs with painted decoration showing paradisiacal motifs are found throughout the quarter. They show variations on flowers, garlands, peacocks, and other birds (Fig. 47; N. Ramage; J. Waldbaum, herein). In most cases the iconography appears to be almost intentionally anonymous— nothing in it would have offended the pagan— and thus the mosaic paving in the apse of the synagogue and the cut marble decoration in the forecourt show that similar motifs of vines, craters of the water of life, and birds held meaning for the Jewish people. The only explicitly Christian tomb is one painted with a Christogram west of the Pactolus near the highway (Butler 1922).

The location of the tombs in relation to the houses and to the churches reflects more clearly the Christianization of the area than does the iconography. The proximity of the homes of the dead to those of the living is a departure from pagan Roman practice which stipulated burials be at a distance from both the civic and the sacred centers. Relics or sacred burials were abhorrent; in fact, a Sardian traveling in Egypt, Eunapius, described the new practices with horror (Brown 1982).

This "Christian quarter" was connected to the main civic center, the gymnasium and bath with the synagogue included within it and a row of early Byzantine shops lining the marble-paved street, by a diagonal colonnaded way that led through the southwest gate in the city wall. A fallen arch with a cross on the keystone may have belonged to a tetrapylon at the intersection with another street lined with columns. The colonnaded way led past houses and shops that descended the terraced hillside to the level of the main east-west thoroughfare.

The area immediately south of the gymnasium, behind the south colonnade along the east-west road and the shops built into it, apparently remained an open space after the earthquake of A.D. 17 until the 5th century A.D. (Hanfmann 1983). Excavation here has revealed units that, unlike most known late antique or early Byzantine houses, were designed and built from the ground up. The units to the east, designated MMS (monumental mudbrick structure) and MMS/S in the site plan (Fig. 7), were built directly over the ruins of the great Lydo-Persian wall (A. Ramage, herein, Fig. 15) with no intervening layers. To the west of these, a large house having a floor of complex marble patterns was built over Roman cemeteries (marked HOB on the site plan). The graves are directly under the floor and one vaulted tomb was carefully preserved under this 5th or 6th century residence.

In the units of MMS one can see the impending transition from Roman to Byzantine housing styles. Apses occur in three units, breaking the rectilinear strictures of Roman house plans (McKay 1975). Open courtyards and peristyles were part of the original design but are encroached upon by the end of the 6th century (Rautman 1986). Painted plaster wall decoration shows motifs of garlands, large crosses, and niches lined with colored stone above which were painted large birds. One apsed unit, perhaps a triclinium, was decorated with panels painted to look like the marble facing of an earlier era. The ceiling, preserved only in fallen fragments of plaster, was deep blue overlaid with rectilinear patterns of gold leaf (Greenewalt 1985). The room could have been used for ritual dining. Although one would expect many churches within the city walls, there is no convincing evidence that any of these buildings were churches.

The colonnades flanking the east-west road on the south side of the bath-gymnasium show three phases of diminishing grandeur. By the early Byzantine period a much reduced colonnade was lined with small shops whose wares and activities constantly intruded on the public space (Fig. 48). The finds in the shops and in the houses across the road also tell much about the transition from Roman to Early Byzantine styles. Liturgical bronzes appear in quantity; the designation HOB derives from the "House of Bronzes," so named because an incense shovel with cross and dolphins, as well as samovars, basins, and censers, were found there (Figs. 54 and 55; Waldbaum, herein). Gilded bronze or brass jewelry with glass inlay was among the items actually made in the shops (Goodway-Vandiver, forthcoming).

Lighting was transformed. A great many glass lamps hung in bronze candelabra and quantities of window glass show a concern for daylight in the interiors of shops and houses. The quantity of glass found was so great that Axel von Saldern (1980) estimates that at least two glass factories were in operation. Glass dishes, bottles, and other vessels complement but never replace their pottery counterparts. Decorated pottery is almost entirely mold-made. The floral motifs of earlier times continue to be popular, but crosses and other Christian symbols appear in quantity on lamps, plates, flasks (Fig. 51), and other utilitarian wares. Holy figures on small flasks, or ampullae, bespeak pilgrimage and piety (Hanfmann 1985). Curiously, no lamps with Jewish symbols were discovered among the hundreds excavated in the synagogue. One lamp showing the sacrifice of Isaac was found in the Byzantine shops and one showing a menorah (Fig. 43) was found in a trash dump that choked the colonnaded street to the south. A great many pieces of pottery and lamps with Christian symbols were discarded in the same deposit of trash. We cannot say where the Jews of Sardis lived in relation to their gentile neighbors, but perhaps the integration seen in the trash heap strengthens the hypothesis that there was no isolated Jewish quarter (Kraabel, herein).

New building in the 5th century city as we know it was confined to churches and the creation of domestic architecture. In the bath-gymnasium and the synagogue, redecoration took place that shows rich painting and gilding, and thin pieces of marble cut in intricate patterns replacing mosaic paving on floors and fashionable on walls set off with red stucco. An arcaded frieze showing birds and craters in this fashion was made to decorate the forecourt of the synagogue. However, a lack of vigor that heralds impending decline is evident in recycled hard-to-work material. When the governor of Lydia wished to give a splendid fountain to the baths, he took one that had previously stood on the main thoroughfare and proudly proclaimed his munificence in an inscription (Yegül, herein).

The 6th century, which saw the bloom of early Byzantine art and culture at the court of Justinian, was a time of decline in the great cities of Asia Minor. At Sardis there is continuous evidence of a tension between public spaces and commercial activity in encroachment on the streets and the palaestra, which by the 6th century had been subdivided and may have resembled an Oriental bazaar more than a classical exercise area. In his researches to the south of the east-west road, Marcus Rautman (1986) sees that the broad colonnaded streets laid out in the 5th century have become blocked with refuse in the 6th and that wells are sunk, indicating the breakdown of the public water supply. It is possible that the area to the south of the bath-gymnasium complex had been abandoned before the end of the 6th century.

When the Christians built their first church it was a smaller version of the basilical plan that had been assumed by the large Jewish community. It is in the 6th century that the diverging fortunes of the two groups is clear in the archaeological record. The forecourt of the synagogue and to some extent the main hall were encroached upon by the shopkeepers, who had also taken over a good deal of the palaestra. Signs of burning could be seen on the mosaic floors. Although it is believed that the synagogue remained in use until the early 7th century (Kraabel, herein), it was much encroached upon. At the same time, Church EA was expanded and a much larger church, D on the site plan (Fig. 7) was built within the city walls, to the northeast.

In the Byzantine shops a lively trade and manufacture continued until the early 7th century. Mortars, pestles, and crucibles were found where they had been used, and coins demonstrate that business was carried on until a massive burning, especially in the western shops, caused their collapse. Of all the Byzantine coins found at Sardis that have been analyzed, about 80 percent were of the 6th century and include a wide range of mints and denominations under the emperor Justinian (527–565; Buttrey 1981). In the shops coins dated 491 to 616 are present in the burned levels, and coin finds over the entire site stop abruptly at the latter date. This numismatic phenomenon, combined with clear evidence for drastic burning and collapse elsewhere in the gymnasium, has led to the conclusion that there was widespread devastation over the site attributable to the raids of the Sassanian Persians under Chosroes II (Bates 1971; Foss, forthcoming). A quantity of arrowheads of an eastern type found at the gymnasium and on the acropolis may also speak for a military encounter (Waldbaum 1983).

There is no historic account of a Persian raid on Sardis during the war between the Byzantine and Persian empires, which lasted from 602 to 627, when Heraklius defeated the Persians at Nineveh. However, Asia Minor suffered tremendously and a conflict at Sardis would have been very likely (Foss 1976; Browning 1980). There is no doubt that Sardis was struck a blow from which she never recovered. The population may well have already been depleted by plague, which ravaged Asia Minor in the mid-6th century. The gymnasium and shops were not rebuilt. The area to the south of them had already been abandoned after only a century of use.

However, no theory of the process of decline of ancient Sardis can be persuasive until excavation of Church D, very possibly the cathedral church of Sardis. If that identification is correct, the major church, originally on the periphery of the western part of the city, had moved to its center, near the Roman theater, stadium, and possibly another bath ("C"; Yegül, herein). Although the unexcavated remains cannot be dated with certainty after the 4th century, there is persuasive evidence that Church D was an imperial project dating to the reign of Justinian (Buchwald, forthcoming). Such large-scale building could have drained the resources of the city (cf. Ephesus, Foss 1979). and the houses and streets in the west may have been depleted as activity centered around the great church farther to the east.

Whether the end was violent and sudden or a century-long process, the fate of Sardis and the world in which she once held pivotal power was set in the later 6th century, "which saw the sad old age of Justinian, the maturity of Pope Gregory I and the youth of Mohammed. . ." (Brown 1982). Although there would be one small glimmer of creative energy in the 13th century, the rising crescent of Islam would find Sardis a meager backwater.

Evidence for the next 500 years is sparse at best. Although Asia Minor returned to Byzantine rule after Heraklius' victory, the great cities never recovered and Sardis seems to have become a military outpost. The very year of Heraklius' triumph at Nineveh, Mohammed moved from Mecca to Medina and began to lay the foundations of an Arab Moslem state. By the death of Mohammed in 632 Arab armies had invaded both Byzantine and Persian territories, and by the 640s the Arabs were in Asia Minor (Browning 1980). There was a lull in the relentless pressure of the Arab raids when the assassination of the caliph Othman in 656 was followed by civil war. Under Constans II (A.D. 641–664) some progress was made in the reconstruction of the cities in the provinces. At Sardis, a new cobbled east-west road was built directly over the ruins of the Byzantine shops, undoubtedly a stretch of a reopened route from the coast inland via the Hermus Valley. The fortification walls on the south side of the acropolis were probably built at the same time, and there is evidence of a settlement within them. A gallery, a gate with a tower, and walls standing about 10 meters high and about three meters thick still stand today. The walls are built of a core of rubble neatly faced with reused stone fragments cut as needed. Brick kilns were doubtless long out of use, and the walls were slammed together with the strongest material at hand from the ruined buildings in the city.

Persians and Arabs were not the only enemies of Sardis in the 7th century. Some time in that century an earthquake loosed a landslide from the acropolis that buried the east end of the temple of Artemis and the little church built there (Figs. 49 and 50). This catastrophe seems to have occurred before the building of the citadel and the new stretch of highway. It may have accounted for the major collapse of the gymnasium and the colonnades along the Roman Marble Road. Building A on the site plan, a large, unexcavated Roman building of unknown date or function, seems to have been spared and strengthened, presumably at the same time, to provide a fortified barracks near the strategic road (Vann, forthcoming). The excavation of Church D could well enlighten the dark period that ensues after the 7th century. Bishops from Sardis attended the Council of Constantinople in 680. Although the church dignitaries may have lived at the capital and rarely visited their see, such population as remained would have been likely to cluster around the great church.

During the 8th century the situation is even more desperate. In 716 the Arabs resumed their attacks and took both Sardis and Pergamon, not only killing and capturing many men but dispersing Syrians living there. Further depopulation would have followed the plague that ravaged the empire in midcentury and left whole towns and villages deserted (Foss 1976). A battle was fought at Sardis in 743 between Constantine V and Artavasdus, during a revolt over the issue of iconoclasm (Foss 1976; Browning 1980).

Under Heraklius a new administrative structure was established which united civil and military rule under a general in one of four *themes* in Asia Minor. The old provinces at first existed as subdivisions of the *themes*, but in the 8th century they were in turn subdivided. Sardis no longer was even in name a provincial capital and was ruled from Ephesus. The old east-west highway was less important than the route farther to the north over which the armies marched from the capital to the east. As a result, the city and its citadel were no longer of much strategic value.

Finally, religious strife in the later 8th century diminished the importance of the large Christian centers. Sardis was in the *theme* controlled by the general Michael Lachanodracon, a fervent iconoclast who tortured and executed or blinded and exiled many monks and persecuted nuns and sold all their holy possessions. The iconoclastic controversy produced a Sardian saint, Bishop Euthymius, who was martyred for opposing the reinstatement of the ban on images in the early 9th century, and there are accounts of other bishops in Lydia who suffered similar persecution (Foss 1976).

Are any of these sad events reflected in the archaeological record? Evidence for destruction in the citadel on the acropolis may well date from the Arab attack in 716 (Foss 1976). Little can be said about the population, but the lack of apparent housing or recognizable pottery in the excavated sectors or on the surface bespeaks depopulation and suggests that those who survived had dispersed to the mountains.

Church EA (Fig. 45) and the sector around it on the Pactolus bank at the western extremity of the city were allowed to fall into total ruin, mute testimony to the religious persecutions. No effort had been made to provide a defense for this church; it remained outside the city wall. One small unit was added on the west, the "West Chapel," some time after the 7th century and before the 11th. However, the main church building seems to have stood empty and by the 9th century it had collapsed.

Although nothing of the cultural and intellectual achievements of the Macedonian dynasty (867–1025) is reflected in the remains at Sardis, the picture brightens somewhat toward the end of the 9th century, probably as a result of Basil I's decisive defeat of the Arabs in 873 and strengthening of the eastern frontier. Church EA was rebuilt with solid walls and piers over the fallen colonnade of the nave. The iconoclastic controversy had subsided and the interior of the rebuilt church was decorated with fresco. Fragments of painted plaster showing flesh tones and extensive bright blue over black are tantalizing indications that there may have been an image of the Virgin, but sadly they are too fragmentary to reconstruct (Buchwald, forthcoming). The capacity for public works may have reemerged. A large cistern built into the ruins of the temple of Artemis may have been constructed late in the century; it contained late 9th century coins. The sequence of coin finds also resumes in the vicinity of Church EA.

The gradual reemergence of life at Sardis suffered many setbacks. There was destruction in the church in the 11th century, probably during raids by the Seljuk Turks who controlled Asia Minor after winning a decisive battle over the Byzantines at Manzikert in 1071. The capital of the sultanate was at Nicaea/Iznik, and Sardis and all of Lydia were ruled from Smyrna/Izmir by Çaka Bey until the Byzantine general John Ducas recaptured Sardis and Philadelphia in 1098 and two centuries of relative peace ensued. Settlements grew up around the cistern at the temple, near the church on the Pactolus bank, to the west of the gymnasium and on the acropolis. Evidence for the manufacture of pottery, tiles, and iron implements has been traced in the gymnasium, in the ruins of "Bath CG" outside the old city walls at the eastern extremity of the area occupied by the Roman city, and possibly on the acropolis. Large, well-made kilns were built into the units of the gymnasium north of the palaestra for firing brick and tile needed for the new houses and, in the early 13th century, for a new church. Brightly glazed pottery that shows both Mediterranean and Syrian influence was used in all these settlements.

Although damaged and encroached upon by graves, Church EA seems to have been in use in the early 13th century, when it was deliberately leveled to make way for a new, smaller church (Fig. 45). In style this church fits well in the first half of the 13th century and historically the most likely time for such a building project would have been during the years 1204–1261, when the Latins held Constantinople and the capital of the Byzantine emperors, the Laskarid dynasty, was at nearby Nymphaeum (Fig. 2), where remains of the palace still stand. Hans Buchwald believes the church can be dated to the reign of John Vatatzes (1222–1254), who spent much time near Sardis and constructed other buildings in the area.

The church stands on a high foundation, which rests on the original subfloor of the Constantinian basilica. The main apse of the new church is set within that of the old and is flanked by smaller apses that close the side aisles, which are separated from the nave by six columns. A central dome on a drum and four pendentives covered the central bay of the naos, and four smaller domes covered the side aisle bays. Only the low portions of the walls were standing, but large fragments of four of the domes and segments of the brick facade that had been violently thrown about when the church was destroyed make it possible to reconstruct the elevation and the patterns of decorative brickwork on the domes and the facades. The decoration includes meanders, chevrons, and checkerboard patterns and lunettes beside the arches of blind arcades decorated with herringbone pattern. This patterning is characteristic of Byzantine brickwork and was further enriched by the light and shadow produced by specially made concave quatrefoils that were set into the mortar (Buchwald, forthcoming).

The interior must have been quite splendid. Glass and gold mosaic cubes were found in the remains. Such sumptuous decoration would have been used only in the main dome or the apse. Remnants of painted plaster can be seen in the smaller domes. Crown glass windows of rose, yellow, blue, and green would have been set in plaster frames. The frames have not survived but a considerable quantity of the glass has and shows that colored glass was used with mosaic, a richness of interior decoration not to be seen in preserved churches (Buchwald, forthcoming).

During the decades of Seljuk control there were mass conversions to Islam (Browning 1980). After the Byzantines regained control, evidence of Christianity is found not only in the church but once again in the small finds. A medallion shows the Anastasis, Christ pulling Adam down to hell on one side and a double cross on the other. Crosses appear in graves and were found in the settlement on the acropolis. One wonders how easily these conversions were made when it was a matter of survival to espouse the official faith and what combination of paganism, Christianity, and Islam might have composed the beliefs of this most embattled population, especially those in the countryside (Trombley 1985).

The building of the small but richly ornamented church on the Pactolus was the last expression of official Christianity at Sardis. It was desecrated and converted to industrial or living space by the 14th century, but there was no evidence that it was transformed into a mosque. Western travelers saw a mosque that had originally been a church, which suggests that a second church was in use when Christian and Byzantine Sardis was reduced to a group of small villages and a caravanserai on the Ottoman road from the coast to the interior.

During the Laskarid period coin finds increase dramatically, all from the mints of Nymphaeum and Magnesia in Lydia. Commerce was again possible and agriculture was restored in the countryside. Refugees from areas controlled by the Latins increased the population, and new villages were built in the region (Angold 1975). But the tide would turn again after 1261, when Constantinople was taken by Michael VIII, who regained the capital and was crowned again in the great church of Santa Sophia but was thereafter threatened on all fronts and lost Asia Minor to the Turks. By the end of the 13th century Sardis was one of a number of Byzantine fortified places in a region otherwise controlled by the Turks. Seljuk control lasted until the end of the 14th century, when Sardis came under the Ottoman empire of Beyazid I (Foss 1976).

It had been many centuries since real power had been centered at Sardis. The interest of the material remains lies in the way they reflect the political and social changes of the last centuries of the Byzantine empire and the rise of Seljuk and, later, Ottoman power. Coin finds stop at the close of the Laskarid period, and silver crusader deniers appear to have been used during a time when bronze coinage was missing. The latest Byzantine coin discovered at Sardis was minted under John V (1341–1391). Thereafter no Byzantine coins mingle with the Moslem issues, but Frankish power in the Mediterranean is reflected in imitation gigliati struck in Izmir which found their way to Sardis. After the Ottoman conquest a steady stream of finds reflects the activity of the market at Sardis until the 18th century, when only small denominations, suitable to the needs of villages, occur (M. Bates in Buttrey 1981).

The pottery reflects an even wider range of culture contact. When the great collections of Chinese celadons were being amassed at the palaces in Constantinople, imitations of their glazes and shapes in earthenware are found at Sardis. Plates and bowls very similar to some found in Syria have been analyzed and were manufactured in western Anatolia, very possibly at Sardis. Their presence gives substance to written testimonia for repopulation (Scott-Kamilli 1981).

After the Turkish conquest the settlements seem to have remained about the same size and in the same locations. The acropolis defenses survived and were used by the Turks, and the cistern in the temple remained in use until the 15th century. The most interesting evidence comes from the village around Church E. Locally made pottery, the archaeologists' staple for assessing culture change, remains unchanged in respect to shape, decoration, materials, and methods of manufacture for 200 years after the Turkish conquest. In the 15th century the bright blue cobalt glaze which appears with the white and local varieties of the wares produced in the imperial kilns at Iznik, was made at Sardis or somewhere nearby. The 16th and 17th centuries bring imports from Iznik, especially two examples of "golden horn ware," which reflect the Ottoman court's taste for Ming porcelain imported from China (Fig 56; Crane in Greenewalt 1977). A 16th century gold ducat struck in the Netherlands and tokens from Nuremberg show that to some slight extent Sardis was in touch with the international trading communities headquartered in Smyrna (Buttrey 1981).

Gregory, the last known bishop of Sardis, may never have visited the place, which was already in Turkish hands. The metropolitan was dissolved in 1369. The only dramatic change that gives immediate witness to the transition from Byzantine to Islamic society is the desecration and reuse of Church E. A small room was added and the church itself was subdivided for use as a dwelling in one part and for a manufactory in another. Layers of ash and large storage jars set into the floor were found by the excavators. The colored glass windows of the church were melted down and used to make Islamic bracelets. Tools— a plane, chisel, and knife— show that other work was carried on there. A Lydian sarcophagus on the north side of the building was used to store water.

The fate of the Christian population is not known. Travelers' reports tell of Greek Christians living in the area through the ensuing centuries, especially at a gristmill. In the 19th century Pliny Fisk, a missionary sent to investigate the state of Christianity in the Ottoman Empire, gives an appealing account of conducting a service at the mill: "We had our forenoon service in the upper part of the mill; and could not refrain from weeping while we sung the seventy-fourth Psalm, and prayed among the ruins of Sardis" (Fisk 1821). This is the last that is known of the congregation at once mighty Sardis which was addressed with such dramatic imagery in the letter of St. John (Rev. 3:1).

The topography and monuments of ancient Sardis retained their identity in human memory and were of great interest to travelers from the west. Sardis was important to them first as the capital of Croesus and second as the recipient of the address in Revelations. Many were merchants, others were chaplains or consuls attached to the trading companies in Smyrna. Their accounts are our best source for the life of the village, Sart, and of the slow disintegration of the ancient buildings, especially the temple (Butler 1922). Many of their reports were published and kept the achievements of ancient Sardis alive in the minds of explorers and scholars in the west before the scientific investigations of Howard Crosby Butler in 1911 and resumed after almost a quarter of a century under George M. A. Hanfmann and members of the Harvard-Cornell expedition which continues the work of unearthing the story of the ancient city. The restored monuments draw a new variety of tourists who, on approaching Sardis by bus or automobile along the route of the ancient Royal Road, are greeted by a sign that reads, "Welcome to Sardis, the most magnificent city of the ancient world."

REFERENCES

Angold, M.
    1975   *A Byzantine Government in Exile: Government and Society under the Lascarids of Nicaea (1204–1261).* Oxford.

Bates, G.
    1971   *Byzantine Coins.* Sardis Monograph 1. Cambridge, Mass.

Brown, P.
    1982   *Society and the Holy in Late Antiquity.* Berkeley and Los Angeles.

Browning, R.
    1980   *The Byzantine Empire.* London.

Butler, H.
    1922   *Sardis. The Excavations.* I, Part I. Leyden.

Buttrey, T. V., et al.
    1981   *Greek, Roman, and Islamic Coins from Sardis.* Sardis Monograph 7. Cambridge, Mass.

Buchwald, H.
    (forthcoming)   *The Churches of Sardis.* Sardis Monograph. Cambridge, Mass.

Erim, K.
    1986   *Aphrodisias: City of Venus Aphrodite.* London.

Fisk, P.
    1821   Visit to Four of the Seven Apocalyptic Churches, *The Missionary Register*, American Board of Missions, October 1821, 428–29.

Foss, C.
    1976   *Byzantine and Turkish Sardis.* Sardis Monograph 4. Cambridge, Mass.

    1979   *Ephesus after Antiquity: A Late Antique, Byzantine, and Turkish City.* Cambridge, Mass.

    1987   Coins, Archaeology and the Decline of Classical Cities in Asia Minor, *Proceedings of the Congress of Numismatics and*

Archaeology, Indian Institute of Research on Numismatic Studies, Maharashta, India.

Goodway, M. and P. Vandiver
A Jeweller"s Shop at Sardis. Draft manuscript. Forthcoming.

Greenewalt, C. H., Jr.
1985   The Sardis Campaigns of 1981 and 1982, *BASOR* Supplement No. 23: 53–92.

Hanfmann, G. M. A.
1983   *Sardis from Prehistoric to Roman Times.* Cambridge, Mass.
1986   The Donkey and the King, *Harvard Theological Review* 78: 3–4: 421–30.

McKay, A. G.
1975   *Houses, Villas and Palaces in the Roman World.* Ithaca, NY.

Ramage, A.
1975   *Lydian Houses and Architectural Terracottas.* Sardis Monograph 5. Cambridge, Mass.

Rautman, M.
1986   The Decline of Urban Life in Sixth Century Sardis, *VII International Byzantine Congress Abstracts of Short Papers.* 285.

Saldern, Axel von
1980   *Ancient and Byzantine Glass from Sardis .* Sardis Monograph 6. Cambridge, Mass.

Trombley, F. R.
1985   Paganism in the Greek World at the End of Antiquity: The Case of Rural Anatolia and Greece, *Harvard Theological Review*, 78: 3–4: 327–52.1.

Vann, R. L.
The Unexcavated Buildings at Sardis, Sardis Monograph. Unpublished manuscript. Forthcoming.

Waldbaum, J.
1983   *Metalwork from Sardis.* Sardis Monograph 8. Cambridge, Mass.

LIST OF ABBREVIATIONS

AJA   American Journal of Archaeology.

AnatSt   Anatolian Studies.

ArtB   Art Bulletin.

BASOR   Bulletin of the American Schools of Oriental Research.

BSA   British School at Athens, Annual.

BSR   British School of Archaeology at Rome, Papers.

CSCA   California Studies in Classical Antiquity.

JFA   Journal of Field Archaeology.

JRS   Journal of Roman Studies.

MAAR   Memoirs of the American Academy in Rome.

Sardis Monograph Archaeological Exploration of Sardis, Monograph. Harvard University Press.

Sardis Report Archaeological Exploration of Sardis, Report. Harvard University Press.

LIST OF ILLUSTRATIONS

All illustrations are courtesy the Sardis Expedition unless otherwise identified.

Title page illustration. Silver stater of the time of Croesus (561–546 B.C.) excavated from the treasury at Persepolis, Iran. Courtesy of the Oriental Institute Museum, University of Chicago. OIM A23052.

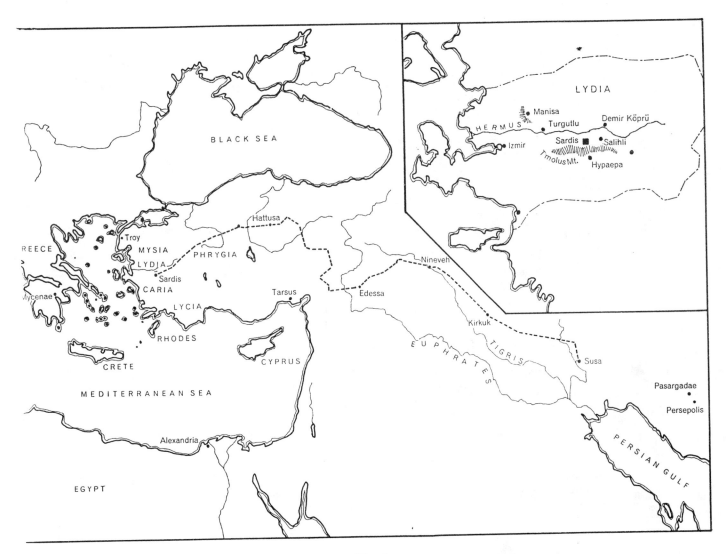

Fig. 1

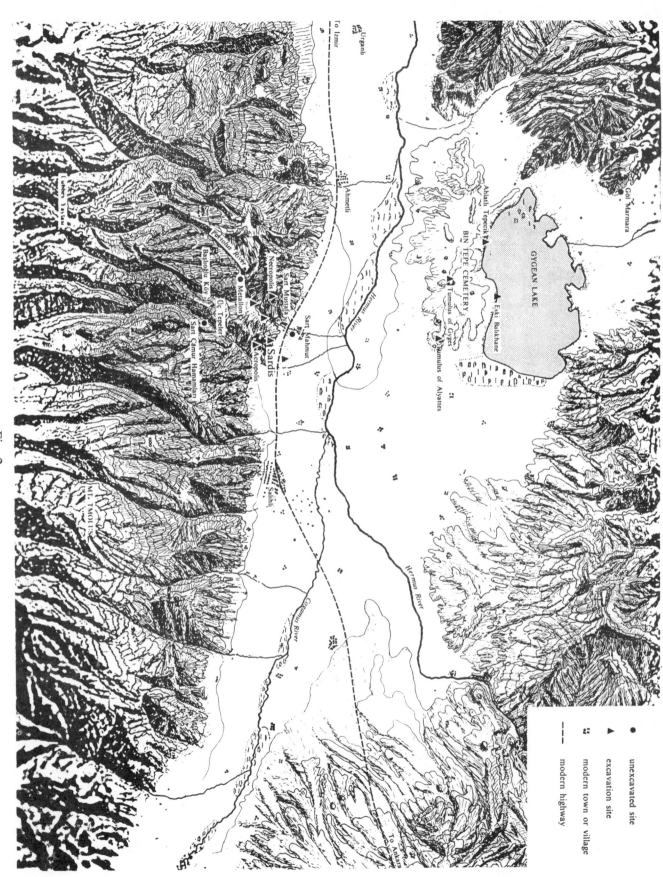

Fig. 2

Fig. 3

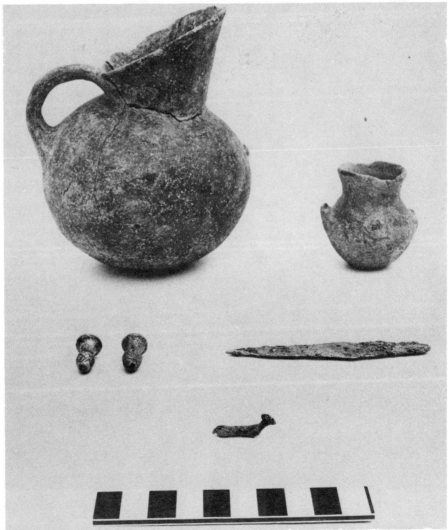

Fig. 4

Fig. 6

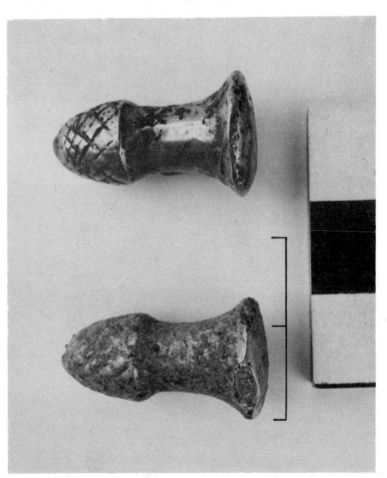

Fig. 5

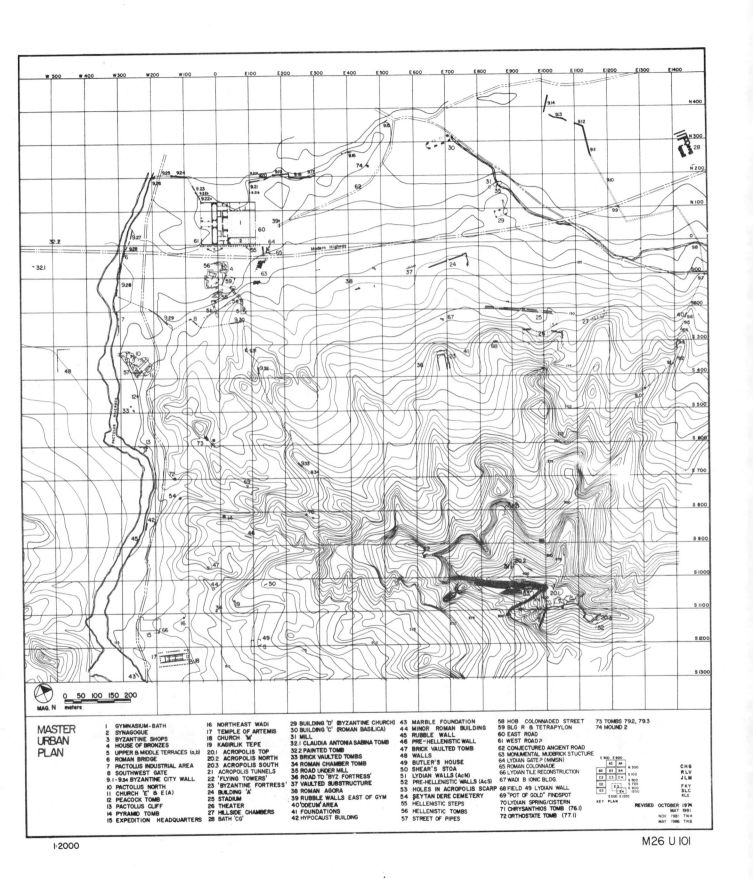

MASTER
URBAN
PLAN

1 GYMNASIUM-BATH	16 NORTHEAST WADI
2 SYNAGOGUE	17 TEMPLE OF ARTEMIS
3 BYZANTINE SHOPS	18 CHURCH 'M'
4 HOUSE OF BRONZES	19 KAGIRLIK TEPE
5 UPPER & MIDDLE TERRACES (a,b)	20.1 ACROPOLIS TOP
6 ROMAN BRIDGE	20.2 ACROPOLIS NORTH
7 PACTOLUS INDUSTRIAL AREA	20.3 ACROPOLIS SOUTH
8 SOUTHWEST GATE	21 ACROPOLIS TUNNELS
9.1-9.34 BYZANTINE CITY WALL	22 'FLYING TOWERS'
10 PACTOLUS NORTH	23 'BYZANTINE FORTRESS'
11 CHURCH 'E' & E(A)	24 BUILDING 'A'
12 PEACOCK TOMB	25 STADIUM
13 PACTOLUS CLIFF	26 THEATER
14 PYRAMID TOMB	27 HILLSIDE CHAMBERS
15 EXPEDITION HEADQUARTERS	28 BATH 'CG'

29 BUILDING 'D' (BYZANTINE CHURCH)	43 MARBLE FOUNDATION
30 BUILDING 'C' (ROMAN BASILICA)	44 MINOR ROMAN BUILDING
31 MILL	45 RUBBLE WALL
32.1 CLAUDIA ANTONIA SABINA TOMB	46 PRE-HELLENISTIC WALL
32.2 PAINTED TOMB	47 BRICK VAULTED TOMB
33 BRICK VAULTED TOMBS	48 WALLS
34 ROMAN CHAMBER TOMB	49 BUTLER'S HOUSE
35 ROAD UNDER MILL	50 SHEAR'S STOA
36 ROAD TO 'BYZ FORTRESS'	51 LYDIAN WALLS (AcN)
37 VAULTED SUBSTRUCTURE	52 PRE-HELLENISTIC WALLS (AcS)
38 ROMAN AGORA	53 HOLES IN ACROPOLIS SCARP
39 RUBBLE WALLS EAST OF GYM	54 SEYTAN DERE CEMETERY
40 'ODEUM' AREA	55 HELLENISTIC STEPS
41 FOUNDATIONS	56 HELLENISTIC TOMBS
42 HYPOCAUST BUILDING	57 STREET OF PIPES

58 HOB COLONNADED STREET	73 TOMBS 79.2, 79.3
59 BLG R & TETRAPYLON	74 MOUND 2
60 EAST ROAD	
61 WEST ROAD?	
62 CONJECTURED ANCIENT ROAD	
63 MONUMENTAL MUDBRICK STUCTURE	
64 LYDIAN GATE? (MMSN)	
65 ROMAN COLONNADE	
66 LYDIAN TILE RECONSTRUCTION	
67 WADI B IONIC BLDG.	
68 FIELD 49 LYDIAN WALL	
69 "POT OF GOLD" FINDSPOT	
70 LYDIAN SPRING/CISTERN	
71 CHRYSANTHIOS TOMB (76.1)	
72 ORTHOSTATE TOMB (77.1)	

REVISED OCTOBER 1974
MAY 1981
NOV 1981 TNH
MAY 1986 TRB

1:2000

M26 U 101

Fig. 7

Fig. 8

Fig. 9

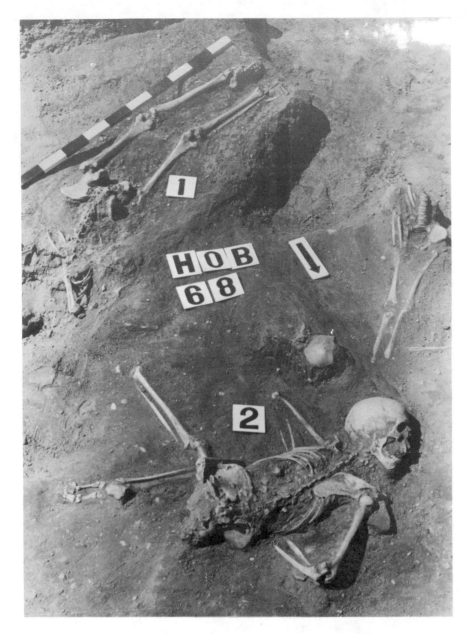

Fig. 10

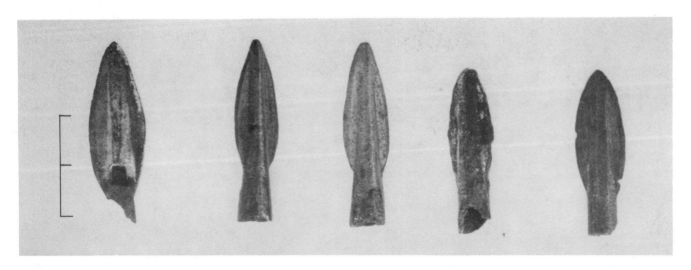

Fig. 11

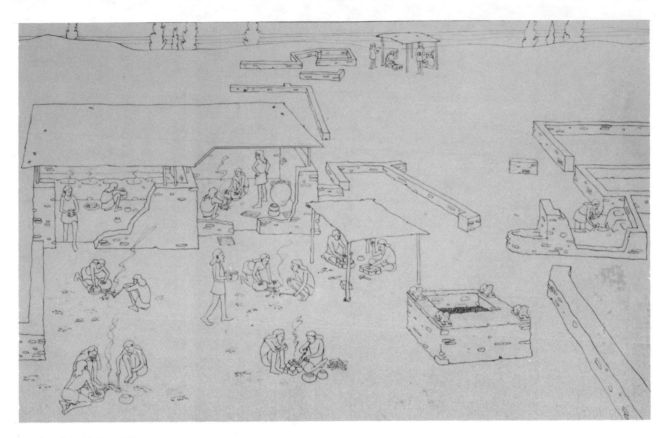

PN 110   LYDIAN INDUSTRIAL AREA
JULY, 1975   E.G.W.

Fig. 12

Fig. 13

Fig. 15

Fig. 14

Fig. 16

Fig. 18

Fig. 17

Fig. 19

Fig. 20

Fig. 21

Fig. 22

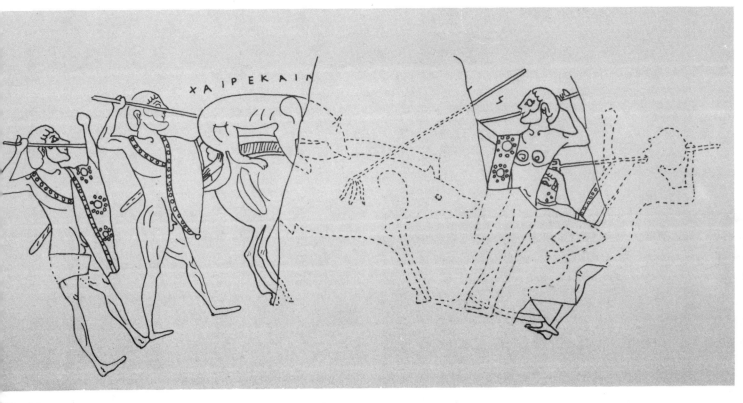

Fig. 23

Fig. 24

Fig. 26

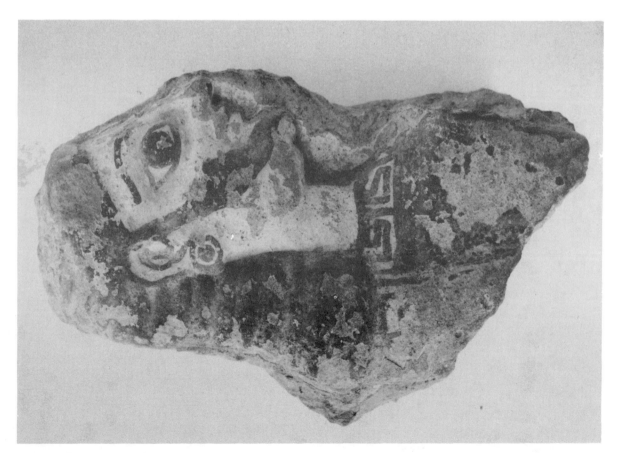

Fig. 25

Fig. 28

Fig. 27

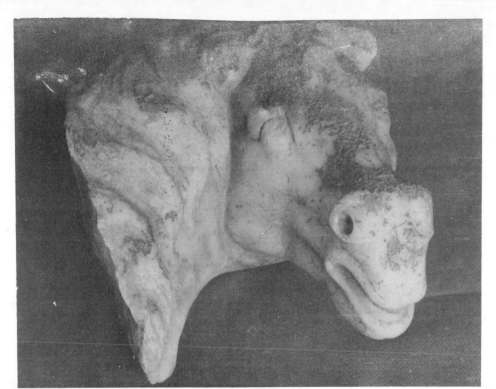

Fig. 29

Fig. 30

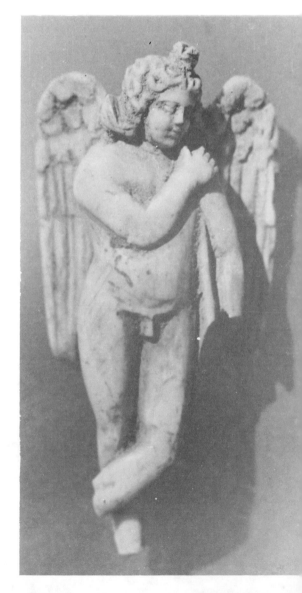

Fig. 31

Fig. 32

Fig. 33

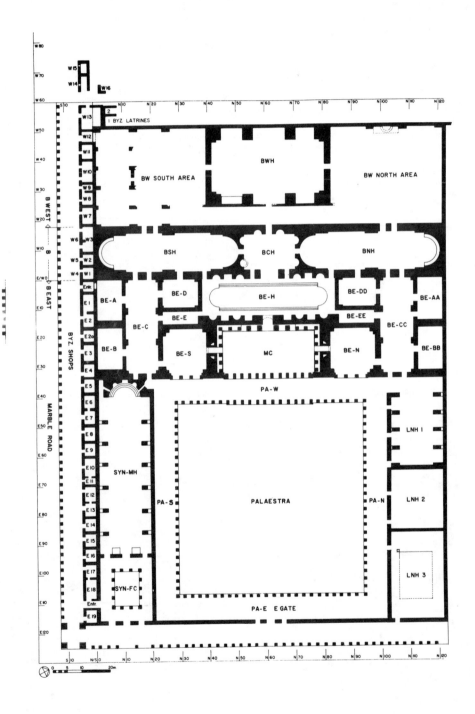

Fig. 34

Fig. 35

Fig. 36

YEGÜL, 82

Fig. 37

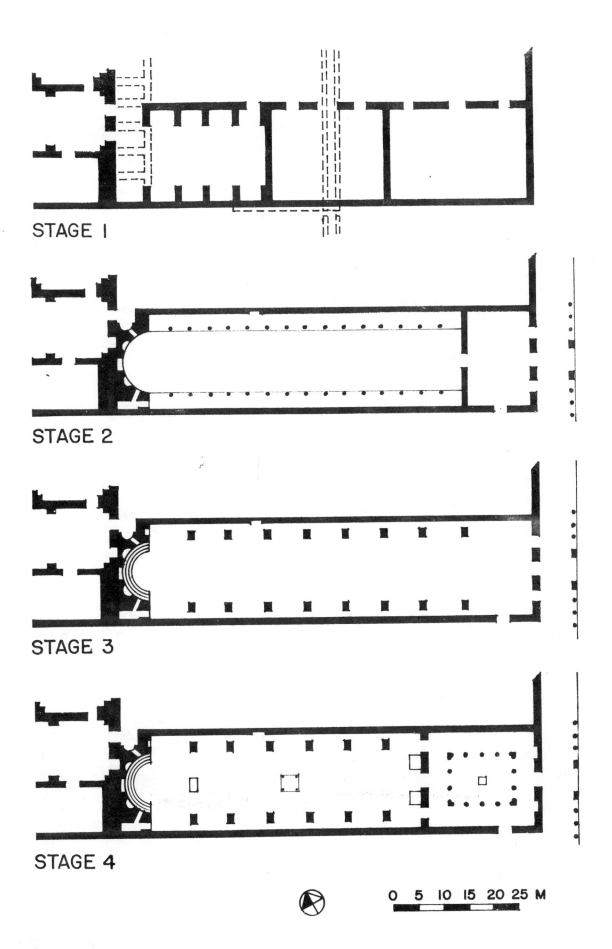

STAGE I

STAGE 2

STAGE 3

STAGE 4

0 5 10 15 20 25 M

Fig. 38

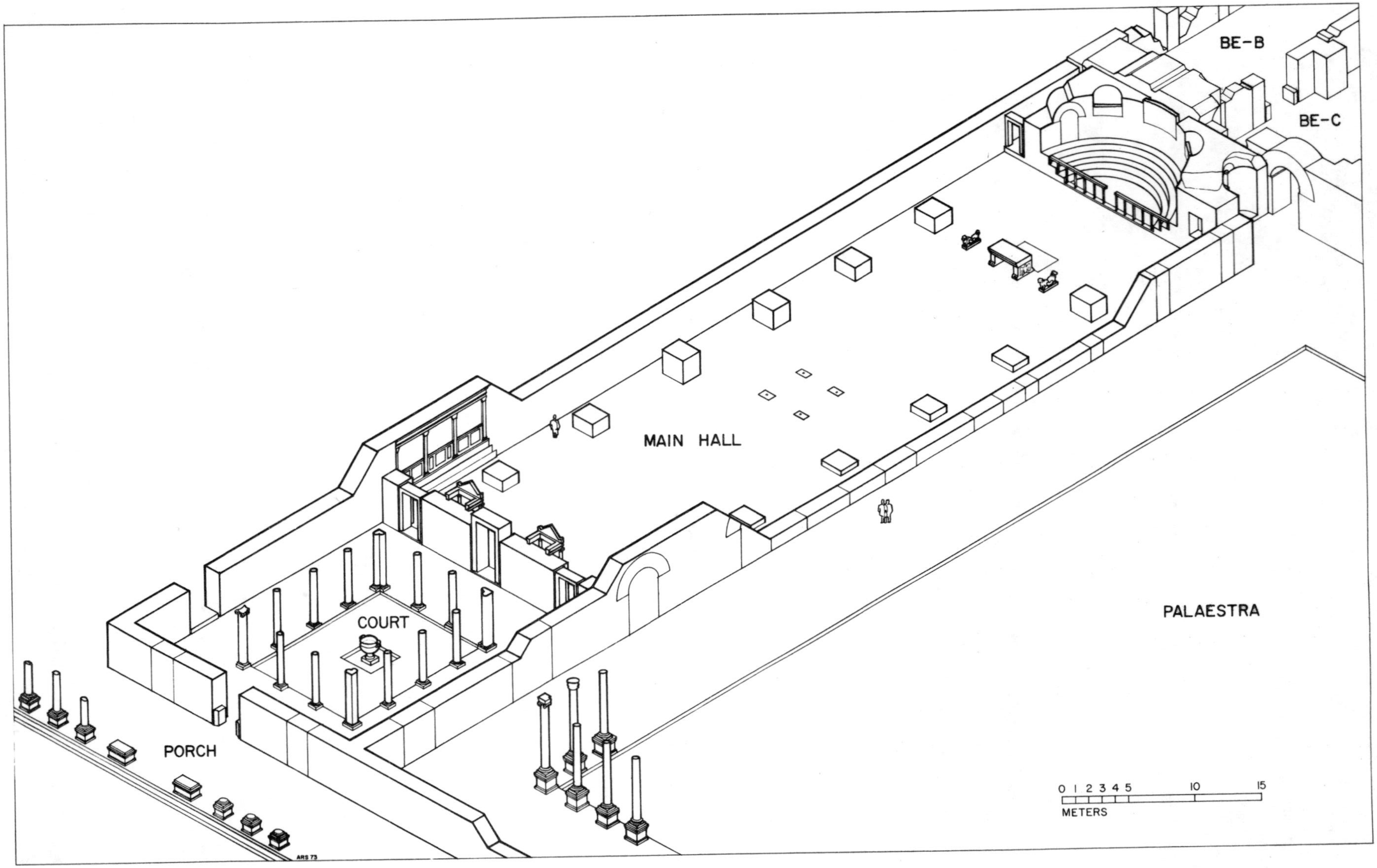

PORCH

COURT

MAIN HALL

PALAESTRA

BE-B

BE-C

```
0 1 2 3 4 5      10      15
|_|_|_|_|_|_____|_____|
METERS
```

Fig. 39

Fig. 40

Fig. 41

Fig. 42

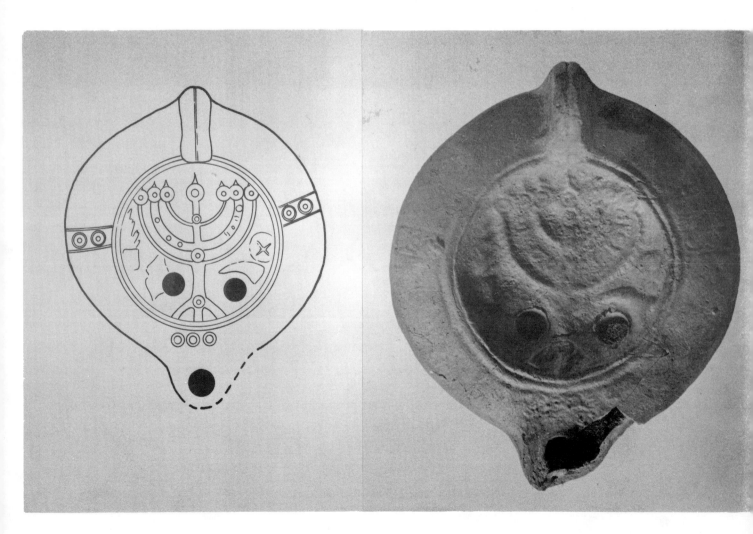

Fig. 43

Fig. 44

Fig. 45

Fig. 46

Fig. 47

Fig. 48

Fig. 49

Fig. 51

Fig. 50

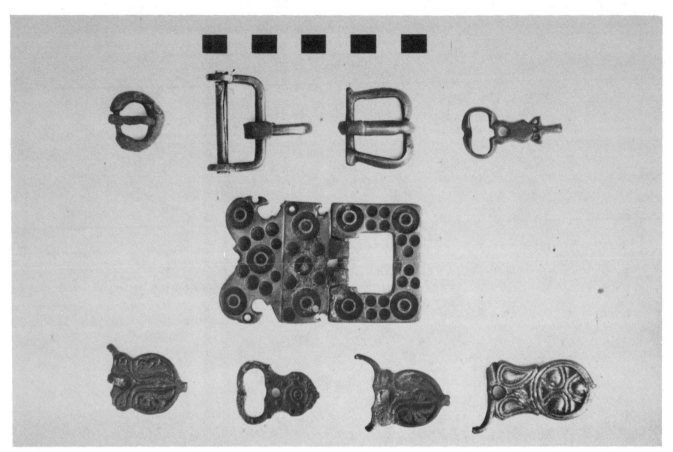

Fig. 53

Fig. 52

Fig. 54

Fig. 55

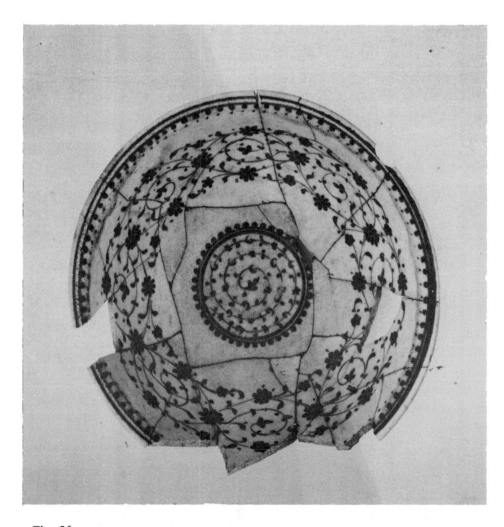

Fig. 56

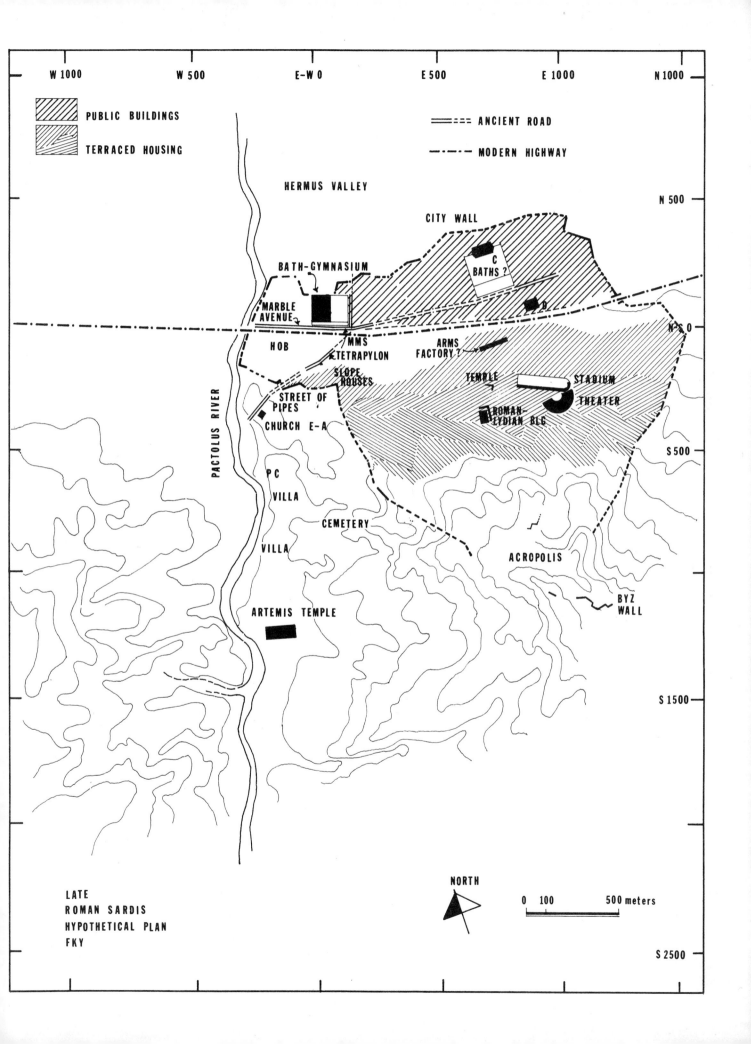

W 1000   W 500   E-W 0   E 500   E 1000   N 1000

PUBLIC BUILDINGS   ANCIENT ROAD

TERRACED HOUSING   MODERN HIGHWAY

HERMUS VALLEY

CITY WALL   N 500

BATH-GYMNASIUM   C BATHS ?

MARBLE AVENUE   D

N-S 0

HOB   MMS TETRAPYLON   ARMS FACTORY ?

SLOPE HOUSES   TEMPLE   STADIUM

STREET OF PIPES   ROMAN-LYDIAN BLG   THEATER

CHURCH E-A

PC

VILLA   S 500

CEMETERY

VILLA   ACROPOLIS

BYZ WALL

ARTEMIS TEMPLE

PACTOLUS RIVER

S 1500

NORTH   0 100   500 meters

LATE
ROMAN SARDIS
HYPOTHETICAL PLAN
FKY

S 2500